EXHIBITION DATES

Peabody Museum, Harvard University
November 8, 1979 to May 4, 1980

Peabody Museum, Salem, Massachusetts
June 1, 1980 to December 1, 1980

Pacific Asia Museum, Pasadena, California
January 18, 1981 to July 13, 1981

CHINA'S INNER ASIAN FRONTIER

Photographs of the Wulsin Expedition to Northwest China in 1923

CHINA'S INNER ASIAN FRONTIER

Photographs of the Wulsin Expedition to Northwest China in 1923

From The Archives of The Peabody Museum,
Harvard University,
and The National Geographic Society

Edited by M. E. Alonso

Historical Text by Joseph Fletcher
Design Editor, Donald Freeman

Published by The Peabody Museum of
Archaeology and Ethnology, Harvard University

Distributed by Harvard University Press

China's Inner Asian Frontier is an exhibition presented by the Peabody Museum, Harvard University from November 8, 1979 to May 4, 1980. The exhibition will then be presented at the Peabody Museum, Salem, Massachusetts June 1, 1980 to December 1, 1980; and the Pacific Asia Museum, Pasadena, California January 18, 1981 to July 13, 1981.

China's Inner Asian Frontier, the catalogue for the exhibition, is published as a book for general distribution under the joint sponsorship of the Peabody Museum, Harvard University, and the Council on East Asian Studies, Harvard University.

This project has been supported principally by a grant from the National Endowment for the Humanities and supplemented by a gift from the Chinn Ho Foundation of Honolulu, Hawaii.

The photographs on the following pages are published here with the kind permission of The National Geographic Society: 17, 29, 39, 42, 44, 56, 74, 75, 77, 79, 81, 82, 83, 84, 85, 86, 87, 88, 94, 96, 97, 98, 99 bottom, 104 bottom, 105 left, 106.

Library of Congress Cataloging in Publication Data
Wulsin, Frederick Roelker, 1891-
    China's inner Asian frontier.

    Exhibition catalog.
1. China, Northwest — Description and travel.
2. Wulsin, Frederick Roelker, 1891-
I. Alonso, Mary Ellen. II. Fletcher, Joseph, 1934-
III. Harvard University. Peabody Museum of Archaeology and Ethnology. IV. National Geographic Society, Washington, D.C. V. Title.
DS793.N6W84   951'.4'041   79-23829
ISBN 0-674-11968-1

Printed by Nimrod Press, Boston, Massachusetts

Acknowledgements

This project was made possible by a grant from the National Endowment for the Humanities, a gift from the Chinn Ho Foundation of Honolulu and the generous cooperation of the National Geographic Society.

I am indebted to a great many people who have helped me in many ways and at various stages; I give thanks to

James Bosson, Sharon Carney, Elaine Chisman, Francis Cleaves, Paul Cohen, Veronica Cunningham, Barbara Curtis, Rodney Dennis, Robert Ekvall, John Fairbank, Wilma Fairbank, Peter Fetchko, Albert Feuerwerker, George Hobart, Dean T. W. Ho, Stuart Ho, David Kamansky, C. C. Lamberg-Karlovsky, David Lattimore, Michael Lattimore, Jonathan Lipman, Raymond Lum, Patrick Maddox, Masatoshi Nagatomi, Claude Pickens, Elizabeth Pickens, Gail Scho, John Schrecker, Thomas Smith, Catherine Taylor, Frank Trout, Ezra Vogel.

Joseph Fletcher's contribution extends well beyond the essay in this volume. His support and advice have been invaluable in all phases of the work. I want to thank Donald Freeman for his sensitive design of this book and the exhibition; Hillel Burger and Christopher Burnett for making such fine prints from difficult negatives; and Daniel Jones not only for his technical assistance but for being so often helpful in so many ways.

I am grateful for the valuable cooperation of the Houghton Library, the Harvard-Yenching Library, and the staff of the Map Room of the Pusey Library.

M. E. Alonso

All captions for the photographs are quotations or excerpts from quotations taken from the letters, notes, and diaries of Frederick R. Wulsin and Janet Wulsin.

Lanzhou

CONTENTS

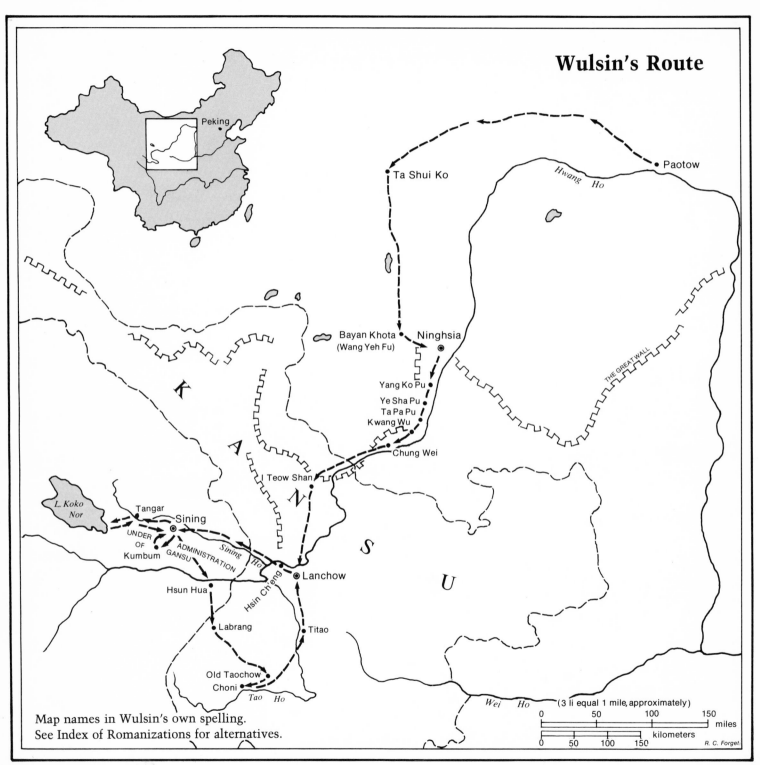

Wulsin's Route

Peking

Paotow

Ta Shui Ko

Hwang Ho

Bayan Khota
(Wang Yeh Fu)

Ninghsia

THE GREAT WALL

Yang Ko Pu

Ye Sha Pu

Ta Pa Pu

Kwang Wu

Chung Wei

K A N S U

I Teow Shan

L. Koko Nor

Tangar

Sining

UNDER OF
Kumbum

ADMINISTRATION
GANSU

Sining Ho

Hsin Cheng

Lanchow

Hsun Hua

Labrang

Titao

Old Taochow

Choni

Tao Ho

Wei Ho

(3 li equal 1 mile, approximately)

0   50   100   150
miles

0   50   100   150
kilometers

R. C. Forget

Map names in Wulsin's own spelling.
See Index of Romanizations for alternatives.

F. R. Wulsin, The Explorer, and the Northwest* China Expedition of 1923

In March of 1923, Frederick R. Wulsin, sponsored by the National Geographic Society, set off on an expedition to the northwest borders of China to collect animal and plant specimens of the region and to build a photographic record of its peoples and places.

Wulsin started his expedition from Baotou in Inner Mongolia. Baotou, which is today a major industrial center, had just become the northern terminus of the Bejing (Peking)-Suiyuan Railroad. It was then a bustling, booming frontier town, spearhead of the centuries-old expansion of Han culture and economic modes into Inner Mongolia. Mongolian nomadic life was giving way to Han cities and irrigated agriculture, and Wulsin recorded this scene and its contradictions.

From Baotou he marched westward in a long arc north of the Yellow River through Inner Mongolia. The members of the expedition were Wulsin and his wife Janet, another American couple, Harry and Susanne Emery, and a Chinese manager, Mr. Wu, two Chinese taxidermists, a botanist, a hunter, a cook, and a groom. As they started out, Janet Wulsin felt their venture into these unknown territories was like a trip to Mars. They rode on twenty-seven camels, six ponies, and a donkey, averaging fifteen miles a day, traveling only in the afternoon and early evening to accommodate the feeding habits of the camels.

The expedition was headed to Wangyefu, the capital of the Mongol kingdom of Alashan, and it took them six weeks to reach it. Their nights were spent in tents, farmhouses, inns, and trading posts. Crossing the Alashan desert, their inexperienced Mongol guide was vague about the location of the water wells, so that they had trouble finding water. Often, after ten hours of strenuous marching, they would find only a well with water so brackish that even the camels

would not drink it. Toward the end of this leg of the expedition, supplies ran low and they were forced to live on millet mush and syrup made from melted sugar.

They stayed a month in Wangyefu, photographing and collecting, then proceeded with six carts (which reminded Janet of prairie wagons) to Lanzhou, capital of the province of Gansu, meeting place of Tibetans, Mongols, and Hans. On mule and horseback they went to Xining and Tangar and to Lake Kokonor, in the Tibetan grasslands. Returning on a southeasterly course, they visited the great lamaseries at Kumbum and Labrang. Here, as in Baotou, they saw societies in crucial transition. In these areas, Tibetan, Mongol, Muslim, and Han peoples and life styles coexisted in a shifting broth. The tides of trade and of the workings of national and cultural interests involved the change from nomadism to settlement, the forming and conflict of ethnic and religious identities, and the jelling of a Chinese nation within the conflicting spheres of influence of world wide empires.

When Wulsin's expedition returned to Lanzhou, they rented a house and gave a Fourth of July party for all foreigners, dining with everyone, including missionaries and civil and military governors, who had given them help along the way. Wulsin also rented an office where he went each day to work on articles for the National Geographic, do accounts and letters, and develop his photographs.

* The official title of the expedition was the Central China Expedition but because of unrest in south and central China Wulsin, in 1923, went to northwest China.

On March 26 as the sun was setting the 27 camels of the [expedition] started for Kansu. You can't imagine what a momentous occasion it was.
F. [Wulsin] dashed about on his small prancing Mongolian pony, equipped for battle in khaki, campaign hat, two guns; the servants were perched on top of various camels looking very ill at ease, Susanne Emery and I were in our "chiaotzus."

J.W. August 1923

We usually travelled about 15 miles a day. Camels have temperament and as they would not change, we had to. They graze all morning from dawn till noon, travel from noon till dark. So we used to have a big meal between 9 and 10 a.m.—a breakfast lunch, which we called "munch" then we carried tea or chocolate and sometimes bacon, which we used to heat up about 5 p.m. riding ahead of the camels and then meeting them when our high tea was over. Supper took place anywhere from 8 p.m. to 11 p.m. depending on the camels, the fuel available, the moon (for if there was one we always travelled late) and the speed of the cook.

J.W. October 1923

From Lanzhou they floated three weeks on a raft down the Yellow River back to Baotou, arriving at the end of October. By now they clearly felt they were heading home. As Wulsin wrote his mother ". . . we have been floating peacefully . . . through gorges where the Yellow River was swift, and dead yellow hills closed us in on both sides; then through level desert, where the stream was slow and we had nothing to look at but now and then a Mongol or his cow . . . we both got well rested . . . I have done a great deal of office work to lighten my load when we get to Peking."

The logistics of such a trip had been formidable, and the planning and management required were clearly pleasurable to Wulsin, who outfitted the expedition with clothing, equipment, emergency foods, personnel, and weapons for every possible contingency; 43 boxes weighing 1,580 kgs. He even carried all manner of receipts and business correspondence going back several years. Some sense may be gained of the logistical magnitude by considering that, by the time they boarded the rafts home on the Yellow River, they carried with them 1,293 zoological specimens and 1,100 botanical specimens, with ten plant sheets for each, in addition to some 2,000 photographic negatives.

It is a testimony to the effectiveness of Wulsin's planning, and perhaps a measure of his luck, that this long trip through little known lands wracked by geopolitical and ethnic conflict, and afflicted by brigandage, was uneventful and in fact without a direct taste of danger.

Wulsin, at this time in his life, was trying to develop a career as an explorer. He had graduated from Harvard in 1913, and done an additional year's study in engineering. In 1914 and 1915 he had traveled in East Africa and Madagascar forming zoological collections for Harvard's Museum of Comparative Zoology. At that time he wrote to his mother "I really think now that this—a mixture of 'scientific exploration,' collecting, etc.—is the work I was born for," and "I see that I have a fair sort of knack at this . . . what I want now is training (say at Harvard in preference . . .) in zoology, botany, geology, anthropology, and practical astronomy, so that when I travel I can do every bit of scientific work that circumstances permit and do it properly."

Chiaotzu. Two small baskets made of a wooden frame covered with blue Chinese cloth and suspended on either side of the camel. You climb in while the camel is on the ground and then he rises or rather unfolds, lurches forward, then back, and is up. But what an arising! The drop in a huge elevator is as nothing compared to it. Ours were the most elaborate, I feel sure, that ever crossed Inner Mongolia. We had spent days interior decorating them, a window of thin Chinese gauze, a curtain to hang down in front and roll up, pockets galore, cushions, a nice fat straw mattress—any small girl would have loved them for a doll house.
J.W. August 1923

For days we slept four in a tent and spent some wild nights while the Mongolian winds shrieked around us and shook the tent as tho' it were made of paper.

J.W. August 1923

After military service in the First World War, he searched about for the basis of the career he envisioned for himself. He decided "to go to China as a scientific traveller, learn Chinese, go into official and other society all I can, and travel through the interior sufficiently to get a thoroughly good idea of it and to make useful scientific records—zoology, meteorology, position and relative altitude observations, some geology and botany if possible—and thorough economic and political and social observations."

Wulsin left for China in 1921. Janet, whom he had married two years earlier, reported to his mother: "F. is full of plans and ideas . . . to get specimens for the museum, to do some work for the National Geographic Society, some data for the State Department, etc.; but when one comes down to brass tacks—all that is definite is the Harvard Museum—who today wrote that they would send him a sum of money to spend as he sees fit. All the rest is vague, possible."

And so Wulsin, whose family had money, in effect, at first financed himself as an investment for the career he had in mind. In 1921 he traveled in the province of Shanxi for five months, and gave the resulting zoological collection to Harvard's Agassiz Museum. He "picked up some germs in Shansi," and spent 1922 in Beijing and the United States recovering. His 1923 expedition, of which this catalogue is a partial record,

was sponsored by the National Geographic Society. The zoological and botanical collections went to the Smithsonian Institution and, after the National Geographic Society chose from among his photographs, he donated the remainder to Harvard's Peabody Museum.

Wulsin's expedition produced approximately 2,000 photographs. The National Geographic Society selected approximately 300 from these and 28 pictures were used to illustrate an article "The Road to Wang Yeh Fu" published in the National Geographic, February 1926. This photographic record has lain quietly for over half a century in the files of both Wulsin and the National Geographic Society, and later, the archives of the Peabody Museum, Harvard University. The negatives are on a nitrocellulose base, which tends to deteriorate, and many have gone beyond retrieval, leaving only positive prints, some of which are of indifferent quality. New prints, made by Peabody photographers Hillel Burger and Christopher Burnett from the old negatives, reveal the fineness of Wulsin's photography.

Wulsin's photographic record is unique. Few people have ever photographed in this part of China. Moreover, since Wulsin's purpose was to thoroughly document the people and their ways of life, the range and detail of his pictorial record are unmatched.

In 1924, accompanied by Captain P. G. Tenney of the United States Army, Wulsin traveled through southwest China, north Vietnam, and northern Laos, again under the sponsorship of the National Geographic Society. Long afterwards, in 1956, he wrote: "The museums were particularly anxious for specimens of this region, but it was a dismal journey for the area had suffered for years from civil wars and famines, with occasional visitations of the plague, and the rains never stopped."

This expedition in 1924 to southwest China was the end of Wulsin's efforts to develop a lifetime career as a professional generalist and scientific explorer. While the model he had in mind was clearly that of the great nineteenth-century explorers, primarily British, geopolitics had changed by the 1920s as had the pattern of sponsorship by the learned societies. The European empires were no longer so much expanding into undeveloped territories as trying to consolidate their holdings, often in conflict with other imperial systems and with national and ethnic stirrings. The sponsorship for exploration and local information now was likelier to come from military and commercial sources rather than from scientific societies. The partial alternative basis of support was journalism, in the manner of Lowell Thomas, where the economics of the mass media complemented the circumstances of modern empires at their borders. Wulsin felt, however, that for him this was not possible because, as he said in the VI Report (1933) of the Harvard Class of 1913, "Unfortunately the gift of descriptive writing is not mine."

We hated to leave [Wang Yeh Fu] but we had to go on. May 31st with six great carts like our old prairie schooners and our six ponies we started for Lanchow.

J.W. October 1923

The carts are broad two wheeled vehicles drawn by four animals. The wheels are about five feet in diameter. All the carts but one have big hooded tops of matting. [They] are costing $108 apiece from Wang Yeh Fu to Lanchow calculated on the basis of 18 days travel at $6 a day. We are to pay $3 a day for each day we elect not to march.

F.R.W. May 1923

Crossing the Yellow River. The ferry is a big ugly flat
bottomed boat of rough boards handled by two
sweeps near the bow and a third at the stern each
with several men to work it. They carry the loads
onto decked portions of the boat, unsaddle the
animals and make them jump on board from
shallow water. On the way over some of them shy
at the swirling waters and rock the boat. The swift
current carried us down several hundred yards, even
so we made the crossing in ten minutes. The horses
jumped out and clambered up a steep bank; the
lightened boat was dragged upstream through shoal
water to its starting point for the return journey and
there the loads were taken off. All our loads and 13
animals went on the first trip, the remaining 4 mules
on the second. We got there at 6:45 and were across
by 10 minutes of 8. The passage of our whole
caravan cost $4.30.

F.R.W. July 1923

Wulsin returned to Harvard in 1925, and obtained his Ph.D. in anthropology in 1929, meanwhile conducting an archaeological expedition to Central Africa. In these years he and Janet were divorced, and he then married Susanne Emery, who had been widowed. In the early 1930s he became a curator for anthropology at the University Museum of the University of Pennsylvania and was involved in archaeological excavations in Iran. During the later 1930s he mainly stayed at home writing and teaching part-time at Boston University. During the Second World War he served in the Quartermaster General's office and did important research on the survival of men under extreme climatic conditions.

From 1945 until his retirement in 1958 he was Professor of Anthropology at Tufts University. There at last this big, vigorous man had a platform from which he conveyed his enthusiasm and his sense of the variety of human experiences and circumstances to a generation of undergraduates. His successor in the large undergraduate course which Wulsin had taught was told by a student: "You may know your anthropology very well and you tell us that these studies are important to a Liberal Arts education, but Professor Wulsin made the lifeways of those distant people seem pertinent to our own lives."

The man who had found no market as an explorer had at last found his audience as a teacher. But he was never a mere colorist; he understood the importance of what he saw. Even as a young man in 1922, while trying to work out the finances for a five-year study of the non-Han peoples and the zoology of China, he wrote: "The Washington Conference and the present civil war in China have made people realize that new political forces are being born in the Far East whose importance for the whole future history of the world it would be hard to exaggerate."

He died in 1961.

M. E. Alonso
Cambridge 1979

Then came six hours of steady plodding over a very winding trail which clung halfway up to the cliff above the [Sining] river.

Crossing this strip of Tibet west of Kansu from the Kokonor country was most delightful. Great grassy plateaux 9,000 to 10,000 feet elevation with wide views of distant mountains, great herds of yak, encampments of black tents of nomad Tibetans, villages of agricultural Tibetans, picturesque lamaseries and an air of the most wonderful freedom. Qinghai.

J.W. October 1923

For three quarters of an hour we marched up the valley bottom, then began to climb a very steep trail that wound through the bushes up the hill on the eastern side. The altitude was 9,300 feet where we left the brook, 11,080 at the top of the ridge which we reached in a little less than three hours' steady plodding.

All was rounded grassy mountain country up on top. We had a wonderful view of round tumbled grey-brown tops in every direction—tops that should have been green but lost their color in the shadow of grey floating clouds.

F.R.W. August 1923

Wulsin with an escort of Muslim soldiers given to
him for his trip to Kokonor by General Ma, the
military commander at Sining. Qinghai.

The eleventh [of October] was better. We should
have made a long distance but instead we celebrated
the good weather by sticking in a mud bank most of
the afternoon.

*The Raft. [We] got all the outfit together, packed the
collections [1293 zoological specimens, 1100 plant
numbers] in great cases which were varnished with
pigs' blood to make them waterproof and on October
6th we got on a raft and came 700 miles down the
Yellow River to Paotow. The raft was unique. We
travelled from dawn to dark and tied up at the bank
at night. Often we made 50 to 100 miles a day, but
as a rule 35 miles was good. It was a peaceful way
to travel except when the winds blew and then we
were tied up to shore and cursed.*

J.W. October 1923

*The raft is built of 72 yak skins, poles and ropes.
Each skin is salted, oiled, and stuffed with straw.
Some air is blown into it with lungs or a bellows
but not enough to get up any pressure. Then all the
openings are tied tight with rope, particularly the
neck opening, which will often go under water. The
leg stumps stick up grotesquely. The skins are
brought into position and lashed together with ropes.
Then timbers are layed lengthwise and across and
the ropes made fast to them. The cross timbers at
bow and stern carry posts for the big sweeps used in
steering. The two end quarters of the boat are
reserved for the crew. The center half is used for
baggage and passengers. We floored one end of the
raft with boards for the tent and the cook house. A
big tarpaulin went over the top and made a big
square tent for the army [Wulsin's men]. The entire
platform measured 28' x 15'. We cast off on Oct. 6
with our regular crew of four men, six extra oarsmen
and a leather-lunged pilot. The walls and hills of
Lanchow faded behind us.*

F.R.W. October 1923

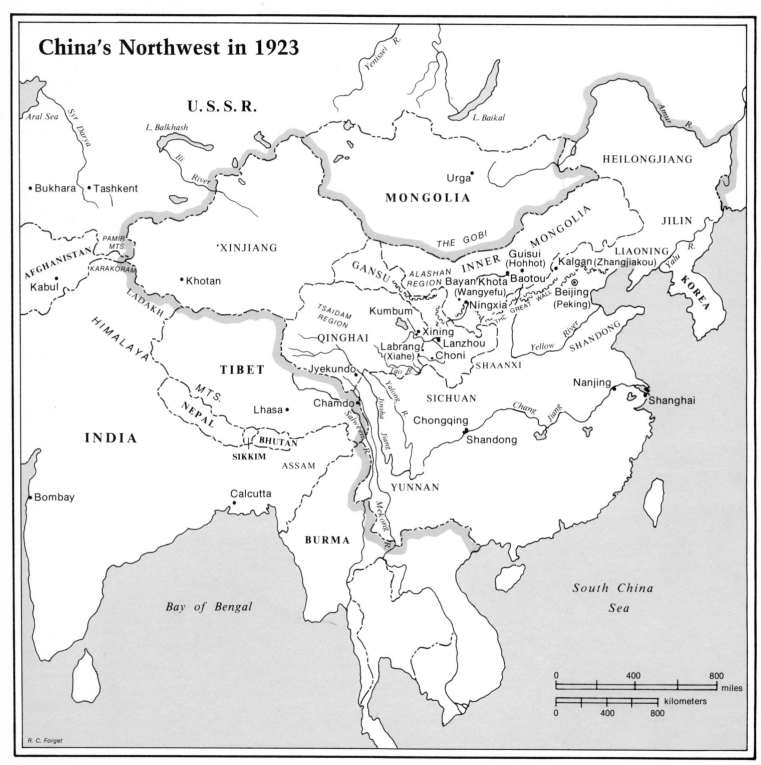

China's Northwest in 1923

Aral Sea

Syr Darya

U.S.S.R.

L. Balkhash

Yenissei R.

L. Baikal

Amur R.

Ili River

HEILONGJIANG

• Bukhara   • Tashkent

Urga•

MONGOLIA

JILIN

PAMIR MTS.

AFGHANISTAN

'XINJIANG

THE GOBI

INNER MONGOLIA

LIAONING

KARAKORAM

Kabul

LADAKH

• Khotan

GANSU

ALASHAN REGION

Guisui (Hohhot)   Kalgan (Zhangjiakou)

Baotou

Yalu R.

KOREA

Bayan Khota (Wangyefu)

Ningxia

Beijing (Peking)

THE GREAT WALL

HIMALAYA

TSAIDAM REGION

Kumbum

Xining

Lanzhou

Yellow River

SHANDONG

QINGHAI

Labrang (Xiahe)

Choni

SHAANXI

TIBET

MTS.

Jyekundo

Tao R.

NEPAL

Lhasa •

Chamdo

Jinsha Jiang

Yalong R.

SICHUAN

Nanjing

Shanghai

BHUTAN

SIKKIM

ASSAM

Salween R.

Chongqing

Chang Jiang

INDIA

Shandong

• Bombay

Calcutta

Mekong R.

YUNNAN

BURMA

Bay of Bengal

South China Sea

0	400	800
miles

0	400	800
kilometers

R. C. Forget

A Brief History of the Chinese Northwestern Frontier

China Proper's Northwest Frontier: Meetingplace of Four Cultures

By Joseph Fletcher

When Frederick Wulsin, his wife Janet, Henry and Susanne Emery, and their team of Chinese helpers trekked from Baotou to Qinghai in 1923, China proper and her northwest frontier stood at the threshold of a new era. China's 2,000-year imperial tradition had crumbled, and her empire had come to an end. A republic, untried and unstable, had replaced it, and no one knew what the future would hold.

The empire's last dynasty, that of the Qing, which had ruled the east Asian subcontinent from 1644 to 1912, had been a dynasty of foreigners, Manchu conquerors from the forests northeast of the Great Wall. They had conquered China, Mongolia, all of eastern Central Asia, and Tibet. At first, to safeguard their territorial base for the control of China, the Qing had closed the areas north and west of the Wall to Chinese immigration. But in time the barriers gave way, and a growing Chinese population expanded outward, bringing about great changes in the lives and cultures of Manchurian tribal peoples, Mongols, Central Asian Muslims, and Tibetans. Although in 1923 the frontier regions were as yet far less affected by Chinese culture and commerce than they are today, they had already begun to reflect China's slowly deepening influence. Since then, the changes there have been rapid, far-reaching, and profound.

Wulsin's photographs of Inner Mongolia, Gansu, and Qinghai capture the life of the southern Mongols and eastern Tibetans on the eve of the unparalleled transformation of the 20th century. His pictures represent the very end of traditional times for two ancient and historically consequential societies, Mongolian and Tibetan, that are now entering the mainstream of Chinese life and are rapidly losing their protective isolation and their sharp individuality. Wulsin has left us the portrait of a disappearing world.

The region through which Wulsin's expedition passed is one of the world's most ethnographically complex. It is the meetingplace of four civilizations: Han (Chinese), Islamic, Turco-Mongolian nomadic, and Bhotia (Tibetan).

Han Civilization

To Americans, the most familiar of these civilizations is that of the Hans, the people whom the English-speaking world generally calls "Chinese." The Hans, who speak various dialects of the Chinese language and have in common a literature that uses semi-pictographic characters instead of an alphabet, populate China proper and represent the overwhelming majority (roughly 95%) of China's population. There are also large, and steadily growing, concentrations of Hans outside China proper, living in that huge and varied peripheral zone known as Chinese Inner Asia (which comprises the Mongolian areas of present-day Heilongjiang, Jilin, and Liaoning provinces; the Nei Monggol Autonomous Region, parts of the Ningxia Hui Autonomous Region and Gansu province, Qinghai province, and the Xinjiang Uygur and Xizang Autonomous Regions).

The origins of Han civilization can be positively identified from as early as the beginning of the 2nd millennium B.C. The heart of Han culture was centered in the agricultural areas of the Yellow River region. In the 3rd century B.C. the Chinese state called Qin conquered the other Chinese states of this region and created an empire that, although sometimes fragmented, was repeatedly recreated and lasted—under various dynasties and with numerous territorial changes—down to the early 20th century. Unable to extend its control beyond north China's agricultural territory, the Qin government connected earlier walls to build the Great Wall of China, separating the Chinese culture area from the steppelands farther north, where nomadic peoples created a different kind of culture.

The Qin empire lasted only sixteen years, but it was succeeded in 206 B.C. by a second empire, named Han, that perpetuated most of Qin's innovations and, in consequence of its long duration (206 B.C.–A.D. 222), firmly established a Chinese imperial pattern. Han, the name of this long-lived empire, became the name of the Chinese themselves and of their culture.

In the 20th century, after the incorporation of Manchus, Mongols, Turks, Tibetans, and many other peoples first within the Republic of China and then in the People's Republic of China (PRC), the term "Chinese" began to be applied to all of China's many peoples. Thus Manchus, Mongols, Turks, and Tibetans all are Chinese, but they are not Hans. The name "Han" refers only to the Chinese-speaking population whose civilization originated in the agricultural regions of north China in the 2nd millennium B.C. At the time of Wulsin's visit in 1923, there was a considerable and growing Han population in Inner Mongolia, but in Qinghai and southwestern Gansu, Hans were still comparatively few. As Wulsin approached Taozhou Old City, for example, heading east through southern Gansu on his way home, he carefully noted that he and his companions "began to see [Han] Chinese farmers" again, whereas to the northwest he had seen some Han woodcutters, but most of the population was Bhotia with only a few Muslim and Han traders living among them.

In Inner Mongolia, on the other hand, Hans were ploughing lands that formerly had been Mongolian pastures. Border cities like Baotou—once lightly populated centers of exchange between Mongols and Hans—had become heavy concentrations of Han population. Wulsin's photographs of the Baotou market, showing an overwhelmingly Han populace, his pictures of Han mummers in a Baotou inn's courtyard, and his portraits of Han craftsmen there plying their trades all reveal the changes that were taking place— the conversion of the southern rim of ethnographic Mongolia into the northern rim of ethnographic China proper. This was a trend that had been noticeably under way since the early 18th century, and in-

A [Han] Chinese tinker. Paotow, Inner Mongolia.

deed Han farmers had cultivated parts of the southern rim of the steppe at various times in earlier history, but by the early 20th century the trend seemed irreversible. There was no denying the facts of population growth. For reasons that are not altogether clear, the Han population was growing at an astonishing rate, forcing farmers to exploit new areas of agriculture if they could.

Wulsin's observations reveal the same process at work in Alashan, at what was then Inner Mongolia's western end. Alashan was ruled by a prince whose family had intermarried with the Qing imperial house. The prince's entourage still dressed like Qing aristocrats and were highly sinicized. The prince himself spoke Chinese but little if any Mongolian. Wulsin estimated that Bayan Khota (Rich City), the spectacularly walled Alashan capital, known in Chinese as Dingyuanying or, locally, as Wangyefu, held a mixed population of from 2,000 to 5,000, and that Alashan as a whole contained about equal proportions of Hans and Mongols. The city lay in an oasis containing suburbs with pools, trees, irrigated fields, and a Han graveyard. It had commercial sections with Han blacksmiths, carpenters, dyers of cloth, and makers of kettles.

Northeast of Wangyefu, Wulsin visited a little farm belonging, he believed, to the Alashan prince's uncle, which was "worked by [Han] Chinese, under the superintendence of a friendly old Mongol." Such farms had existed earlier in Inner Mongolia under the tacit protection of the Qing dynasty, but by Wulsin's time their number and economic importance had grown. He also observed that Alashan Mongols had a monopoly on bagging the salt from the pits between Baotou and Wangyefu and on carrying it by camel to Dengkou, whence it was floated down the Yellow River to be sold at Baotou, and other Chinese cities. At a frontier trading post north of the river he also observed that the Mongols bought Han-produced cloth, tea, sugar, iron, and brassware, but, interestingly, little grain.

Islamic Civilization

Also familiar to Americans is Islamic civilization, although the broad extent of Islam's influence outside the Middle East, and in China in particular, is little known. This category is a mixed one, because it comprises a large number of ethnolinguistically different peoples who share only their Islamic religion and various aspects of a common Islamic civilization. The size of the Muslim population in China defies close estimation. Figures run from as low as 10,000,000 to as high as 50,000,000.

The most numerous Muslim people in China goes by the name of Hui, which once simply meant "Muslim" but now more specifically designates the Chinese-speaking Muslims, who are descended mainly from Hans converted to Islam since the 16th century. The Huis speak the same Chinese dialects as the Hans and are divided from them essentially only by religion; yet the Huis have always tended to regard themselves as a separate people. The size of the Hui population remains unknown and perhaps unknowable, because political caution may have prompted a considerable proportion of the Huis to register themselves as Hans. Official PRC estimates now put the Hui population at almost 4,000,000,

Wangyefu, Inner Mongolia.

23

but the Republic of China's official estimates from the 1930s estimated China's Muslim population at about 48,000,000. Most of this figure was accounted for by Huis.

Despite their linguistic and other similarities, the Hans and the Huis have had a bitter history of mutual friction and war, especially in what is today the Ningxia Hui Autonomous Region, Gansu, and Qinghai—precisely the region through which Wulsin passed. "The Moslems and the [Han] Chinese fight freely on occasions" even at Lanzhou, the Gansu provincial capital, he noted in his journal, "usually stabbing frays that rise from some small quarrel. I got the impression that the province is a rough one, with plenty of people who hanker for trouble, but that ordinary civil commotion is restrained through fear in each party, [Han] Chinese and Moslem, that the other will attack if a good opportunity presents itself."

Han-Hui relations were particularly hostile in the 18th and 19th centuries, when the Qing government in effect supported the Hans against the Muslims, and Qing suppression of Muslim "rebellions" left a legacy of resentment. In some places, such as the long eastern suburb of Xining, where the Hui population had been massacred in the 1895 Muslim uprising, Muslims reestablished themselves once again. Lanzhou, for example, had suburbs full of Muslims on every side except toward the Yellow River, but Huis shied away from heavily Han-dominated cities like Zhungwei, where Muslims remained highly unpopular. "The [Han] people resisted them successfully during the rebellion," Wulsin was told, "& do not care for them now." Both sides had practiced barbarities. In the Ningxia region Wulsin saw "towns which are mere empty shells" after being "sacked by the Mohammedans." The Muslims may have been a minority "even in their own districts," but, Wulsin wrote, they "have such vigor, initiative, cohesiveness and taste for fighting that they give the tone to a considerable region."

These tense conditions did not, however, create Hui solidarity. The Muslims of the northwest had many differences among themselves, and some of them sided with the Qing against their fellow Huis. After the collapse of the Qing dynasty in 1912, the Beijing government was no longer able to repress the Huis of China proper's northwest frontier or to maintain the old imperial ban on foreign travel. As a result, Hui local warlords took power for a while in western Inner Mongolia (especially the Ningxia region), Gansu, and Qinghai, acting in the name of the Republic of China; and many Huis made the pilgrimage to Mecca, studied at centers of Islamic learning in the Middle East, and returned to China, bringing with them new schools of Islamic thought and practice. Factions proliferated, and factionalism has remained a fact of Hui life. At Taozhou Old City, for example, Wulsin noted that "most of the people are Mohammedans of the 'new new sect.' They are building a big new mosque in the suburb."

Although an overwhelming majority of the northwest frontier's Muslim population is Hui, there are also the Turkic-speaking Salars, whose boatmen virtually monopolized water transport on the upper reaches of the Yellow River in Wulsin's time, and who, in the vicinity of Xunhua in Qinghai, where the largest concentrations of Salars are to be found, seemed to him to be "a Mohammedan agricultural tribe." Unlike the Turkic-speaking Uighurs of Xinjiang, whose relations with their Hui co-religionists were in general uneasy, the Gansu and Qinghai Salars seem to have got on fairly well with the Huis.

China has many other Muslim peoples, but the only other sizable group of Muslims in the vicinity of Wulsin's expedition was the Bhotia (Tibetan) Muslim community, most of whom had embraced Islam in the 18th century. In the present-day Xinjiang Uygur Autonomous Region the largest Muslim nationality is the Uighurs (Uygur) who number about 4,000,000. Kazakhs, Kirghiz, Tajiks, Uzbeks, and Tatars also add to the number of Xinjiang's Muslims.

Turco-Mongolian Nomadic Civilization

The third civilization on China proper's northwest frontier is that of the Turco-Mongolian nomads. The name of the Turks is included in the term because the early Turks, who dominated the Mongolian steppe in the 6th century A.D., developed steppe nomadism in its final form, the form in which the Mongols later adopted it. Many of the Mongols' cultural traditions and patterns of life can be traced back to these early Turks.

Mongols' herds of camels and flocks of sheep and goats. Alashan Desert, Inner Mongolia.

After the Mongols conquered the entire steppe in the 13th century, the Turks mostly disappeared from Mongolia and were eventually converted to Islam. The present-day Mongolian People's Republic (MPR), the Xinjiang Uygur Autonomous Region, and Qinghai have nomadic Muslim Turkic-speaking Kazakh populations, whose nomadic culture—apart from its religious element—closely resembles that of the Mongols. Xinjiang also has a substantial number of Muslim Turkic-speaking nomadic Kirghiz. But in the regions where Wulsin and his party traveled, the Mongols were the sole representatives of Turco-Mongolian nomadic civilization.

The Mongols presently number fewer than 2,000,000 in the PRC, to which may be added about 1,000,000 in the MPR and several hundred thousand more in the USSR, plus a tiny Mongolian remnant in Afghanistan.

Their nomadic style of life, which they inherited from previous steppe peoples, the Turks, Xiongnu, and Scythians, was adapted to support human life on grasslands and the sparse vegetation of the Eurasian steppe. Unlike the nomads of the Middle East, who have traditionally been part of a nomad-sedentary continuum in which pastoralists live near and in close cultural and economic interdependence with urban and agricultural populations, the nomads of Mongolia have lived a highly separate existence from the Chinese agricultural world to the south of the Great Wall of China. Interaction was possible and common on the frontier between the Mongolian and Chinese worlds, but east Asian geography is such that the two worlds did not greatly overlap. Two separate civilizations have therefore developed, and the separation between them began fully to break down only a few decades before Wulsin made his trip.

Nomadic life was hard. The Mongols had to keep their livestock, upon which their economy was predicated, moving all the time, for the animals quickly consumed the vegetation. Everybody went—men, women, children, the young and the old. People were born, married, fell sick, and died, all on the move. They could not stop. The Mongols lived in felt tents and dressed themselves in leather and survived winter cold of 40° or more below zero and terrible winds. They ate meat, drank milk, and in desperation could quench their thirst by tapping a horse's vein. They believed in a shamanist world of spirits who intervened in human affairs. They worshipped fire. They practiced human sacrifice, until, beginning in the 16th century, Tibetan Buddhism changed their religion and weaned them away from it.

In war they could sleep in the saddle and go for many days and nights without camping for rest. They cultivated the martial arts: horsemanship, archery, wrestling, and the hunt. They raided one another, tribe against tribe, realm against realm, and composed heroic sagas, which they sang to the accompaniment of the horse fiddle. When times were hard, and sometimes when they were not, they raided the Hans, and

Nomadic Mongols in the Alashan desert.

they never forgot the great days of the Mongolian empire in the 13th century when they conquered them, and much of the rest of the world.

As a result of their incorporation into the Qing empire in the 17th century, the eastern Mongols came for a while to be administratively divided into two main imperial territories: Inner Mongolia, south of the Gobi desert, and Outer Mongolia to the north of it. Various western groups of Mongols, known as Oirats (or, in Russia and among the Turks, as Kalmuks), lived in Xinjiang and Qinghai. Another, northernmost group of Mongols, the Buriats, lived in the forested areas of southern Siberia, and these now dwell in the USSR.

Linguistically, Mongolian—the language of the Mongols—belongs to the family of languages known as Altaic, to which the Turkic and Manchu-Tunguzic languages also belong. Many scholars assign Korean to the same family, and some add Japanese. Mongolian has numerous dialects and much regional variation, but for the most part these differences are not so radical as to prevent communication.

Bhotia Civilization

The other civilization on the northwestern frontier of China proper belongs to the Bhotias (Tibetans), whose mountainous, isolated tranquility, Buddhist philosophy, terrifying religious art, and distinctive architecture have long captivated the Western imagination. At their greatest extent in the high middle ages, the Bhotias controlled an immense but sparsely populated zone that stretched over what is now Tibet proper (the Xizang Autonomous Region), present-day Qinghai, half of Sichuan, much of Yunnan, Gansu, and southern Xinjiang, both sides of the Himalayas, including Assam, Bhutan, Sikkim, large portions of Nepal, the north Indian frontier areas, Ladakh, the northeastern part of present-day Pakistan, and the Pamirs. Today Bhotia populations still live in all of these regions.

In all, the Bhotias may number about 4,500,000, of whom some 3,000,000 live in Tibet, the name given to the Bhotia territories lying within the boundaries of the PRC. Tibet proper corresponds to the Xizang (a Chinese name for central Tibet) Autonomous Region, consisting of the historical Tibetan provinces of Ü, Tsang, Ngari, the western part of the easternmost Tibetan province of Kham, and also the western half of the empty northern pasture zone called Changthang. Eastern Kham is now under the administration of Sichuan province. The northeastern Tibetan province of Amdo is now the Chinese province of Qinghai ("Blue Lake," Kokonor in Mongolian), named for the large Lake Kokonor in the northeast corner of the province, where Wulsin's expedition spent much of its time.

The Bhotias' language, Tibetan, belongs to the Sino-Tibetan family of languages, which also includes the Chinese language of the Hans, but within each of these two languages there are dialect differences of such magnitude that Hans of different regions cannot understand each other, and various Tibetan dialects are also mutually unintelligible. Speakers of Chinese in Inner Mongolia, Gansu, and Qinghai, however, all use one or another subdialect of Mandarin, so that communication between them is possible in a way that it would not be with, say, speakers of one of the Chinese dialects of the south China coast. Differences between the Tibetan dialects, on the other hand, are more extreme, making communication difficult if not impossible between some of the region's Tibetan groups.

The Tibetan population of Qinghai and southern Gansu, where Wulsin visited, is highly varied, consisting mainly of farmers, nomads, monks, and traders. "West of the Moslem region," Wulsin noted, "one comes to the Kokonor territory, a high plateau of grass lands sparsely inhabited by nomad Tibetans. Tibetan farmers, similar in race, live in the border valleys wherever the altitude falls below 10,000 feet and agriculture is possible." Locally, Mongols referred

to all Bhotias, nomad or sedentary, as Tanguts (the name of a northeast Tibetan kingdom that flourished in the 11th and 12th centuries), and Hans and Huis referred to them as Fanzi, an ancient Chinese name for Bhotias. The Bhotias themselves made a distinction between *Bod-pa* (Bhotias) *par excellence,* namely the agricultural population, and *'brog-pa* (pastoralists), namely the nomads. Tibet, in other words, was viewed as being quintessentially agricultural.

Most of Amdo's agricultural population inhabited the region of the southern Gansu-Qinghai border and was subject to the prince of Choni (Co-ne), an old settlement, situated in Gansu on the upper course of the Tao River, possessing its own distinctive dialect of the Tibetan language, which Wulsin described as "very peculiar." Traditions ascribe Choni's founding to soldiers from Tibet proper in either the 8th or the 10th century, but a local tradition says that the Choni population did not come there from Tibet proper until shortly after 1368, when the rule of the Mongols collapsed in China. The principality of Choni, most powerful of all the lay chieftaincies of Amdo, was hereditary and vested in a lineage that traced itself back to a Lhasa family sometime in the 13th or 14th century. From the 18th century on, Choni's small monastery distinguished itself as one of four main centers where the Tibetan Buddhist canon was printed from wooden blocks.

In Wulsin's day the "pastoralist" element of the population predominated as far east as the great Buddhist monastery of Labrang (Bla-brang), lying just outside Qinghai, within the provincial borders of neighboring Gansu. "The language one hears on all sides," Wulsin reported, "is Drocwa ['brog-pa] Tibetan, and he who knows only Chinese feels a stranger in a strange land." Many of the Bhotia tribes were, so Wulsin was told, "as wild as they could be." In southern Gansu there were "48 wild tribes," subject to the prince of Choni, who were "wild in more than one way, disobedient and given to raiding and stealing." The prince, Wulsin said, "keeps them in check and occasionally has run a punitive expedition against them." Another Bhotia tribal people with a fearsome reputation were the mGo-log, who lived a highly independent life in southeastern Qinghai.

In addition to agriculture, pastoralism, and various trades, monasticism occupies an important segment of the Bhotia population, just as lamaist Buddhism dominates Tibetan cultural life. Apart from a comparatively small number of Tibetan Muslims, Tibet is a solidly Buddhist region, adhering to a highly Tibetanized form of Buddhism, heavily intermixed with remnants of Tibet's pre-Buddhist priestly religion (called Bon) and other traditional religious elements. There are several different monastic orders, or "churches," but the most important is the dGe-lugs-pa, or Yellow Church. To this order belong the two most important monasteries of Amdo, namely Kumbum (sKu-'bum), south of Xining, and the monastery of Labrang in Gansu, as well as the much smaller one at Choni, all three of which Wulsin visited.

The Kumbum monastery, historically Amdo's most important, is one of the largest in all Tibet. By 1577 some monks' cells, a temple, and a "tower" enclosing a miraculous lilac, said to have sprung from the placenta (or, as Wulsin was told, the first hair cuttings) of Tsong-kha-pa (1357–1419), founder of the Yellow Church, had been built at Tsong-kha-pa's birthplace in northeastern Amdo. In 1582 the third patriarch of the Yellow Church—the first patriarch to bear the title of Dalai Lama in his own lifetime—founded a school there for scriptural studies, and over the course of the 17th century Kumbum developed into a major monastery, eventually dominating the region. When the Kumbum lamas supported a rebellion against the Qing empire in 1723, the Qing army burned the monastery, scattering and killing its monks, but later the Qing government contributed to its reconstruction. Kumbum's architecture is therefore more Han than Bhotia in style, and most of its principal monks have been Monguors (a local Mongolian-speaking people called Turen in Chinese) rather than Tibetans. Kumbum, the seat of a reincarnating lama who was understood to be Tsong-kha-pa's father, recognized the Dalai Lama's religious primacy but remained autonomous in ecclesiastical and secular administrative matters. Under the direct jurisdiction of the military authorities at Xining the monastery governed and taxed the pastoral tribes and agricultural villages in its vicinity.

The history of the Labrang monastery is less well known. It was founded in 1709 by Ngag-dbang brTson-'grus, a famous exegetical scholar whose works continued to be used as prescribed texts at Labrang until the mid-20th century. Like Kumbum, Labrang became the residence of an incarnate lama ('Jam-dbyangs-bshad-pa, the founder's reincarnation); it was an important place of pilgrimage and one of Tibet's largest monasteries. Labrang governed and taxed many agricultural and nomadic groups. The economic importance of its trading village (now called by its Chinese name Hexia) stemmed from its function as the first entrepot in the wool and hides trade from Tibet to China proper. In Qing times Labrang was in Xining prefecture of Gansu province, and at the time of Wulsin's visit it was under the protection of Xining's Hui commander.

Wulsin found Labrang particularly arresting. Geographically, as he put it in his journal, "Labrang falls naturally into two parts, . . . the monastery full of monks and the village full of merchants and pretty Tibetan girls" (he crossed out this last phrase). Socially, it consisted of three parts, "the monastery, the village, and the Mohammedan garrison." "A roadway," he wrote, "leads from the village to the temple and beyond. On it there is a ceaseless stream of lamas, pilgrims, hucksters, townsmen, idlers, soldiers and peasants, up to the temple and down again." Noting the practice of exposure of the dead, he explained that the "dead lamas' remains are devoutly fed to the vultures," and that a market was held every morning, where "the belongings of dead lamas, and all manner of odd wares, are likely to come for sale."

Of the Labrang trading village he said, "Its architecture has no charm, but its population has: a medley of lamas, wild tribesmen, [Han] Chinese fur buyers, Mohammedan soldiers, and richly dressed Tibetan women with magnificent straight figures and white sheepskin hats. Many live by their charms. It is a sight to see others, in never ending procession, bring up tall wooden buckets of water from the river on their backs."

Through Buddhism and its monastic orders the Bhotia and Turco-Mongolian cultures have become increasingly merged, especially since the missionary efforts of the Yellow Church among the Mongols in the 16th century, and nowhere more than along China proper's northwest frontier. Here it would have been possible in Wulsin's time to speak of a Tibeto-Mongolian culture, for Tibetan culture was present and obvious everywhere among the Mongols, particularly in the domain of religion. A high proportion of Mongols bore Tibetan names.

Monks at the Labrang Lamasery, Gansu.

The monasteries housed monks, most of whom were Bhotias, but who also included many accomplished Mongols. In their monastic garb Bhotias and Mongols were indistinguishable. They worshipped in buildings that were indistinguishable by architectural style, built similar stupas, spun similar prayer wheels, participated in similar temple dances, sounded similar long-stemmed trumpets, and put votive stones and prayer-flags on similar shrines. Many monks, although Mongols, were literate only in Tibetan and regarded Mongolian writing as *khara*—"black," profane, and unworthy. Yet monks and lay people lived in close association with one another.

Among the laity, Bhotias and Mongols were more easily distinguished. The peaked hats of the Tibetan nomads were not the same as the Mongols' headgear. The elaborate hairstyles of the Tibetan women, which varied from one locality to another, had something in common with the distinctive hair dressings and ornaments of upper-class Mongolian women; women's fancy gowns, caps, and shoes bore certain resemblances, but there were differences too.

The yak, originally a Tibetan animal, had long since made its way into domestic use in Mongolia, and Mongolian and Tibetan nomadism had many points in common. But the hemispherical Mongolian felt tent differed strikingly from the black tents of the Tibetan nomads (which Wulsin described as "big square black affairs with many poles outside, covering a great ground space"), betraying a basic difference in the origins of nomadism in Mongolia and Tibet. Mongolian nomadism was developed in the Eurasian steppe. Tibetan nomadism, however, had its origins in the Middle East and is related to the black-tent nomadism of the Arabs, Pashtuns, and others in the broad zone stretching from north Africa to Pakistan and Afghanistan.

We met a herd of yaks loaded with baggage in bales and leather sacks, coming down to meet us. Three horsemen in fleece lined gowns with bare shoulders and swords in their belts were herding them along pell mell. The men were of the Djekwur tribe on their way home with grain for which they had traded wool at Tangar. They told me the yak carry 120 catties each; and I take it this is a maximum load. The yak wears a miniature pack saddle which looks ridiculously small on his great frame when the load is off. Each yak wears a wooden triangle in his nose. These beasts are not led but driven in a disorderly herd by men who use shouts, blows and stones to direct them. Their march is slow, perhaps 40 or 45 li [15 miles] a day. But they can live altogether on grass and withstand the worst weather in admirable fashion. Qinghai.

F.R.W. August 1923

The Nomads of Mongolia: a Historical Sketch

The nomadic culture of Mongolia arose in the western half of the Eurasian steppe sometime after the domestication of the horse about the beginning of the second millennium B.C., over 3000 years before the Mongols themselves appeared in the historical record. Eurasian steppe nomadism evolved from primitive Near Eastern agriculture and entered history as the way of life of various Indo-Iranian-speaking groups who are referred to collectively as Scythians. Eventually other peoples too borrowed the techniques of Scythian nomadism, and among these were the mighty Xiongnu (evidently a cognate of the name Hun), who created an empire in the Mongolian steppe that rivalled and at times dominated the Han empire in China, south of the Great Wall. What language the Xiongnu spoke is still a matter of dispute, but it seems not to have been Iranian. Perhaps it belonged to the family of Paleosiberian languages spoken by the Kets and others of the Yenissei River valley, or, more probably, it may have been Altaic. Whatever their language, the Xiongnu adopted merely the nomadism of the Scythians and some aspects of their culture but were themselves a completely different people.

From that time on, until the 17th century, when the Manchus conquered both China and Mongolia and began to weld them together under a single rule, the nomads of Mongolia and the agriculturalists of China confronted each other as two separate, mutually hostile worlds. But because of their propinquity, their histories remained heavily intertwined. When China's unity under the Han dynasty gave way to a period of divison in the 3rd century A.D., the unity of the Xiongnu also collapsed. In the 4th and 5th centuries, when a tribal people from Mongolia known as the Tabghach (Tuoba in Chinese) conquered and unified north China, founding a kingdom known as the Northern Wei, another tribal people, called the Ruanruan, conquered the steppe and unified it under a new nomadic realm. In the 6th century, when the Turks (known as Tujue in the Chinese sources) once again united the Mongolian steppe under a single nomadic rule, the Chinese Sui and Tang dynasties, in which Turkish cultural influences also played an important role, similarly reunited China under a reconsolidated empire.

By the early 10th century, China and Mongolia were each once again in a state of fragmentation, but another nomadic people, known as the Khitans or Khitays (whence Kitai, the Russian name for China, and the English name "Cathay"), began to assert their control over parts of Mongolia and the Manchurian forests. The Khitans, whose ruling house is referred to in Chinese as the Liao dynasty, spoke a language that most scholars believe to have been a form of Mongolian. They annexed a strip of north China, including the site of the present Chinese capital, Beijing, founding the forerunner of that city. In the rest of China a corresponding political reintegration occurred under the Song dynasty (960–1126).

It can be seen that down to this time peoples from Mongolia had heavily influenced Chinese history. The Northern Wei dynasty was of Inner Asian origin, and the Sui and Tang ruling houses were of mixed ancestry. Some of the founders of Chinese kingdoms in the period of disunity before the Sui-Tang empire and in the political disintegration before the Song were non-Han "foreigners" from Inner Asia. The Khitans, a non-Han people, controlled a northern zone of Chinese territory inside the Great Wall.

But in the early 12th century something happened in China that had occurred only once before, under the Northern Wei. A Manchurian forest people known as the Jurchens overthrew the Khitans and invaded the Song empire, forcing its government to flee to the south, where it reconstituted itself as the Southern Song (1127–1279). Thus, for the second time, the northern half of China fell to a foreign invader. The Jurchens created an empire in southern Mongolia, Manchuria, and north China under a ruling house called in Chinese the Jin, or "Gold," dynasty (1126–1234) and established, in sharp contrast to the Song, an essentially military government that reduced civil bureaucrats to the role of functionaries. The administrative structure of the Jin empire was based on a mixture of precedents drawn from the Khitans, from Jurchen traditions, and from Chinese patterns of administration.

Finally, in the early 13th century, the Mongols made their appearance. They were a nomadic people whose culture resembled that of the nomadic Turks who had dominated Mongolia before the rise of the Khitans two centuries before. Originally the Mongols had been a hunting people of the Siberian forests, but at some point—it is unclear when—they had moved from the forests into the steppe and adapted themselves to the pastoral nomadic way of life that had been developed by the Scythians, Xiongnu, and Turks.

Unlike the Khitans, who had gained familiarity with agricultural civilizations from their long domination of the northern Chinese frontier, the Mongols were as wild as or wilder than any nomadic people that the Chinese had yet encountered. Their khan, whose personal name was Temüjin but who is better known under his title of Chinggis Khan (later corrupted into Genghis, Jenghiz, and other such forms), directed the Mongolian armies against the Jurchen empire in north China, which at that time was probably the strongest power anywhere in the world—apart from the Mongols themselves.

Among the nomads, monarchy had always been highly personal rather than bureaucratic. Political cohesion depended upon the person of the ruler and commonly dissolved when he died because there was no custom of primogeniture, levirate, or other orderly principle of succession. The breakup of the realm after a ruler's death had generally limited the growth of nomadic kingdoms, but Chinggis Khan succeeded, surprisingly, in passing on his empire more or less intact to his third son and chosen successor, Ögödei.

The empire was known to the nomads, who thought first in terms of people and only secondarily in terms of territory, as the Yeke Mongghol Ulus (Great Mongolian Nation). It stretched from Korea to eastern Europe and from the Siberian forests to the northern fringes of India, and its capital was at Karakorum in the northern part of the present-day MPR.

Ögödei continued the wide-ranging campaigns of expansion that his father had begun. In 1234 the Mongols overpowered the Jurchen empire and conquered all of north China. After Ögödei's death in 1241, which saved western Europe, the unity of the Mongols' world empire weakened. The descendants of Tolui, Chinggis Khan's youngest son, replaced the house of Ögödei on the throne in eastern Asia. In Russia and the western steppes, the descendants of Jochi, the eldest son, ruled as effectively independent sovereigns. But the Mongols' territorial expansion continued. Tolui's son Hülegü invaded the Middle East, captured Baghdad in 1258, and ended the Abbasid caliphate, an event of vast repercussions for subsequent Islamic and Middle Eastern history.

In China, Tolui's son Möngke led campaigns against the Song until his death from dysentery in the south, which was followed by a succession dispute between two more of Tolui's sons, Arigh Böke and Khubilai (the Kubla Khan of Coleridge's poem). Khubilai won, completed the conquest of China, and sent armies into Southeast Asia, including a naval expedition into Indonesia. He established his winter capital at the approximate site of present-day Beijing and created a China-based empire, adopting the dynastic name of Yuan. As seen through the eyes of subsequent official historiographers, the Yuan empire conformed to China's traditional political system, but in fact it was based on Mongolian institutions combined with the north China administrative system that the Mongols had inherited from the Khitans and Jurchens. This the Mongols extended to cover all of China, obliterating the Song dynasty's more Chinese and Confucian traditions. It was this Khitan-Jurchen-Mongolian system that the Han-Chinese Ming dynasty would eventually inherit in 1368 and would perpetuate in China, rather than the traditions of the Song.

By basing his empire in China, Khubilai lost the support of the more nomadically-minded Mongols in the steppe, and he soon faced a renewed succession war in Mongolia against the house of Ögödei. The struggle was not resolved in Khubilai's lifetime, and even after the Yuan triumphed over their rivals in Mongolia at the beginning of the 14th century, the Mongols in China never succeeded in joining China and Mongolia together as complementary components of a single politically integrated state. This remained for the Manchus to do in the 17th and 18th centuries.

A Brief Glance at Tibetan History

From its earliest origins the Bhotia (or Tibetan) world seems to have consisted of agriculturalists, specialized in the growing of barley and other high-altitude crops, and the raisers of livestock—nomads who pastured their animals in the high open places where agriculture was impracticable. Speaking several dialects of Tibetan, the Bhotias were gradually integrated by a common culture, in which Buddhism came to be a principal ingredient. Buddhism, which came from India, brought with it various aspects of Indian civilization, the most important of these being the alphabet, which made possible the development of a supra-dialectal Tibetan literary language, further accelerating the process of cultural integration.

Precisely dated historical personalities begin to appear in Tibet proper in the first half of the 7th century A.D., when King Srong-btsan sGam-po conquered Tibet's northeastern province of Amdo as far as Lake Kokonor and was strong enough to force the Tang-dynasty Chinese emperor to give him a princess in marriage. He also married a Nepalese princess, and because both women were Buddhists, his reign was a period in which Buddhism along with Chinese and Indian cultural influences made a considerable impact in Tibet. In the latter half of the 7th century, the Tibetans conquered the oases of what is today the southern part of the Xinjiang Uygur Autonomous Region and overran the Nanzhao kingdom (a Thai people) in present-day Yunnan. In 763 the Tibetans, allied with the Uighur Turks, invaded the Tang empire, captured the Chinese capital, and replaced the Tang emperor on the throne with a candidate of their own choosing. In the late 8th century Buddhists built a complex of temples in central Tibet, following an Indian architectural model, and toward the end of the century the king established Buddhism as the official Tibetan religion. Rivalry between Indian and Chinese Buddhist schools of thought finally led to a debate in which the Chinese teachers lost and were forced to leave the country.

In the 9th century, Tibetan society passed through a period of confusion and political disintegration. Anti-Buddhist forces came to the fore, and the Tibetan kingdom lost control over many of its peripheral territories. To escape persecution, some Tibetan Buddhists emigrated to Tsong-kha, another Tibetan kingdom in the region of present-day Xining, where Buddhism continued to be the official religion. Here Buddhist monks gathered also from Khotan, in today's southern Xinjiang, which had recently been incorporated within the orbit of Islam. In central Tibet Buddhism made a comeback in the 10th century, and from then on it dominated the cultural life of the Tibetan world.

Meanwhile a third Tibetan kingdom known as Minyag, called Tangut in Mongolian and Xixia in Chinese, arose on Tibet's northeastern periphery. Its capital was situated on the Yellow River at Ningxia. Although scholars have generally ascribed its language to the Tibeto-Burman branch of Sino-Tibetan, the language of the ruling house seems to have been Altaic, and it has been suggested that literary Minyag was a language of Altaic origin too. In 1038 the Minyag king declared his independence of the Song empire and carved out a sizable empire for himself in northwest China and Amdo, conquering Tsong-kha in 1068.

Throughout Tibet Buddhism flourished, and native schools of religious thought and practice began to proliferate. In the late 11th and 12th centuries Tibet witnessed the founding and rise of most of its famous monastic orders—bKa'-gdams-pa, rDzogs-chen-pa, bKa'-brgyud-pa, Sa-skya-pa, and their various branches. These acquired both spiritual and temporal power, each dominating particular regions and sending missionaries throughout the Tibetan world and into the lands beyond. Each order acquired secular patrons, allying itself with local aristocratic families. Monasteries recruited their own military forces and played politics. Some of the orders became, in effect, regional ecclesiastical states.

Distribution of Mongolian, Muslim, and Bhotia population (1923)

U.S.S.R.

Lake Baikal

Lake Balkhash

HEILONGJIANG

MONGOLIA

JILIN

INNER MONGOLIA

LIAONING

XINJIANG

KOREA

GANSU

Lake Kokonor

QINGHAI

Yellow River

TIBET

SICHUAN

Chang Jiang

YUNNAN

	Mongols
	Bhotias [Tibetans]
	Muslims

0   500 miles

0   500 kilometers

R. C. Forget

The Confluence of Tibetan and Mongolian History

The sudden rise of the Mongols in the 13th century soon carried the missionary efforts of the Tibetan monastic orders far beyond the borders of Tibet. Chinggis Khan sent raiding parties into Amdo as early as 1206 and 1207, and in 1209 his forces besieged the capital city of Minyag, which promptly surrendered. Later, when Minyag failed to supply Chinggis Khan with military forces, the Mongols turned on Minyag and utterly destroyed it in 1227 in a campaign during which Chinggis Khan died. In their subsequent expansion, the Mongols conquered large parts of Tibet and extended their political hegemony over most of the Tibetan-speaking world.

In China the Mongols proved resistant to Chinese culture, but Tibetan Buddhism excited their interest. They patronized Tibetan monks, giving them a place at court, where the Buddhism of Tibet functioned as a high-culture counterweight to Chinese traditions—something the Mongols were unable to match by drawing on their own traditions from the simpler nomadic life of the steppe. Soon lamaism became the dominant religious force among the Mongols in China. Tibetan cultural prestige is further to be seen in the Mongols' efforts to legitimize their rule by becoming secular donors to various Tibetan lamaist orders, which provided the Mongols in return with religious blessings and sanction. The emperor Möngke became donor to the Karma-pa order, a branch of the bKa'-brgyud-pa. Möngke's brother Arigh Böke made himself donor to the Tshal-pa order, another branch of the bKa'-brgyud-pa, in order to win support for his struggle against his brother Khubilai, who was donor to the Sa-skya-pa order. Hülegü, a fourth brother, the conqueror of Iran, became donor of the 'Bri-gung-pa order, yet another branch of the bKa'-brgyud-pa.

In Tibet the Mongols' hegemony was loosely felt. Khubilai's seizure of power in east Asia initially gave the Sa-skya-pa order a pre-eminent place in Tibetan politics, but the geographical realities in mountainous Tibet prevented the Sa-skya-pas, for all their Mongolian patronage, from undermining the regional powers. By the end of the Yuan dynasty in 1368, several different monastic orders, in alliance with local aristocratic families, ruled the separate regions of Tibet as independent states.

It is common wisdom that China's Han civilization always conquered China's conquerors, but for the Mongols this seems not to have been true. When a Han Chinese revolt drove the Mongols back into Mongolia in 1368 and established the Ming dynasty, the Mongols seem to have been fully as Mongolian and nomadic as they had been over a century and a half earlier when they first invaded north China. The main addition to the Mongols' culture that resulted from their residence in China was Tibetan Buddhism, and this the Mongols took with them when they returned to the steppe. The Ming dynasty, on the other hand, encouraged some groups of Mongols to settle in north China and gave them employment in various military capacities. Contacts between Mongols and Hans in north China's cities, dating from the Yuan period, were thus uninterrupted down to the 20th century. But most of the Mongols remained surprisingly little influenced by Han Chinese culture until the 18th century, when the Qing empire would incorporate them within a sinicized, China-based realm.

From the late 14th to the 17th centuries China and Mongolia led separate and, for the most part, mutually hostile existences. The Yongluo emperor of the Ming mounted several campaigns into Mongolia in the early 15th century and destroyed Karakorum but failed to do serious damage to the Mongols' military strength. In the middle of the 15th century the Oirats (Western Mongols) captured the Ming emperor in battle but sent him home again when it became clear that the Chinese would make no concessions to get him back. Thereafter the Mongols alternately raided the Chinese borders and traded at Chinese frontier markets. Eventually commerce became regularized as "tribute," which the Mongols presented to the Ming emperor. This was, of course, a fiction. The Mongols' raids forced the Ming government to permit the nomads to trade with China.

In the 16th century, strong Han influences began to be felt among some of the Mongolian tribes who lived closest to the Chinese frontier. Altan Khan of the Tümed Mongols encouraged Han refugees and renegades to settle within his domains and to open farms on suitable patches of land. He established a capital city named Bayishing in southern Mongolia near present-day Hohhot, and the immigrants, fugitives, and captives from China—like Mongols who had been encouraged to settle south of the Wall by the Ming—interacted with the nomads, trading influences. On both sides of the Ming-Mongolian border a few impoverished Mongols gave up nomadism and began to live in villages and to engage in agriculture. In the 20th century, the Tümed were among the most highly sinicized of all the Mongols.

Although Tibetan Buddhist influence had been weakened somewhat by the Mongols' return to their nomadic life of the steppes in 1368, there is plenty of evidence that lamaism continued to play an important part in Mongolian life of the late 15th and early 16th centuries. But missionary efforts by the Yellow Church in the late 16th and early 17th centuries brought about a great Buddhist revival across the entirety of the Mongolian world.

At the beginning of the 15th century, a monk known as Tsong-kha-pa because of his birth in the region of Tsong-kha, had founded the dGe-lugs-pa, a new branch of the bKa'-gdams-pa order, as a reform movement emphasizing monastic discipline. Following a practice already in use among the Karma-pas, the principal lamas of the dGe-lugs-pa order were claimed to be reincarnations, so that they were regularly rediscovered in children born shortly after an incarnate lama's death. The dGe-lugs-pa movement, referred to as the "Yellow Church," became increasingly influential, absorbing other monastic orders as it spread through central and eastern Tibet. But it provoked the resistance of the Karma-pa order, which allied itself with the 'Bri-gung monastery and the aristocrats of the province of Tsang.

The struggle between the Yellow Church, based in the province of Ü, and the Karma-pa, which came to be referred to as the Red Church, based in Tsang, soon dominated Tibetan politics. Both sides, following the precedents of the 13th century, sought supporters among the Mongols. The Yellow Church found military allies among the tribes of southeastern Mongolia, and in 1578 Altan Khan of the Tümed held a meeting at Lake Kokonor with the incarnate dGe-lugs-pa patriarch and formally embraced the Yellow Church, giving the patriarch the title of Dalai Lama. (Dalai literally means "sea," which renders a corresponding Tibetan epithet in the titles of all the dGe-lugs-pa patriarchs. This epithet has connotations of "oceanic," meaning "all-embracing" or "universal.") From this time the Yellow Church spread rapidly throughout Mongolia, gradually displacing shamanism, the Mongols' indigenous religion that had coexisted with earlier forms of Buddhism from Tibet. In 1601 the Mongolian-Yellow Church alliance was cemented by the formal recognition of Altan Khan's great grandson as the Dalai Lama's next incarnation, and when a Jurchen power in Manchuria, known as the Manchus, extended its hegemony over much of southeastern Mongolia it too joined the alliance, further strengthening the Yellow Church's position.

The Red Church, a coalition of orders headed by the Karma-pas and supported by the princes of the province of Tsang, having enjoyed contacts with the Mongols from at least the late 15th century, sought out Mongolian allies of their own. In the early 17th century the Red Church made common cause with some of the Khalkhas (northern Mongols) and with the powerful ruler of the Chahar tribe named Legdan Khan, a descendant of Chinggis Khan. The alliance was a natural one, because Legdan had imperial ambitions, and the Manchus, aligned with the Tümed and other tribes and with the Yellow Church, stood as the chief obstacle to his aims. For a time Legdan Khan and the Red Church held their own, but by the 1630s Yellow-Church influence had thoroughly permeated the Oirats, and the Oirats' Khoshuud tribe in eastern Tibet also joined the Yellow Church alliance. The balance swung sharply in the Yellow Church's favor. Legdan Khan set out on campaign against the Yellows, but he contracted smallpox and died ten day's march from Lake Kokonor in 1634. The ruler of the Khoshuud, Güüshi Khan, took military control of northeastern Tibet in the name of the "Great Fifth" Dalai Lama in 1637, then proceeded to conquer Tibet for the Yellow Church in the years immediately following. He uprooted the Red Church's power and proclaimed the Dalai Lama religious and secular ruler of all Tibet in 1642.

The Qing Dynasty in Inner Asia

The Manchus, having secured their control over the eastern Mongols at the death of Legdan Khan, invaded China in 1644, seized Beijing, ended the Ming dynasty's rule, and established the empire of the Qing dynasty—the Chinese-style name of the Manchu ruling house. The Manchus essentially perpetuated the imperial system of the Ming dynasty, which, with a few noteworthy changes, was itself basically the Yuan imperial system, adapted from the Jurchens who had in turn adapted it from the Khitans. Just as the Jurchens had earlier insisted that all their subjects wear the Jurchen clothing and hairstyle, the Qing made a few specifically Manchu customs official practice for the empire, the most notable of these being the Manchu shaved forehead and queue (pigtail). Except for noblemen, who were included within the Manchu aristocracy, the Mongols, as allied subjects, were exempted from wearing the queue, but the Hans, who were conquered subjects, had to comply.

Soon after subduing most of China proper in the 1640s, the Manchus broke up the tribal structure of their Mongolian allies, so as to render them incapable of independent collective action, and reorganized them into smaller units, called "banners," each of which was directly answerable to the Qing government. In this way the Manchus extended their effective administrative authority over all the southeastern Mongols, creating a territory of the Qing empire that they referred to as Inner Mongolia. Outer Mongolia, the home of the Khalkhas, still remained outside Qing control, but in the 1680s and 1690s the Manchus skillfully intervened in the troubles that had arisen between the Khalkhas and a northern group of Oirats known as the Zunghars, so that when the Zunghars invaded Outer Mongolia the Khalkha princes fled south and placed themselves voluntarily under the protection of the Manchu emperor. Once again, the Manchus broke up the tribal structure, divided the Khalkhas into "banners," and annexed Outer Mongolia as a territory of the Qing empire.

In Tibet, the Yellow Church functioned as the effective government, but military power remained in the hands of the Oirats of the Khoshuud tribe in the region of Lake Kokonor. Oirat politics continued to dominate Tibet in the late 17th and early 18th centuries. The Zunghars, in an effort to counterbalance the Manchus' influence in the Mongolian world, invaded Tibet in 1717, but the Manchus responded in the name of the child Seventh Dalai Lama, who had been residing at the Kumbum monastery. In 1720 a Qing army escorted the Dalai Lama to Lhasa, thus winning the support of most of the Tibetan people, and the Zunghars were forced to flee.

Installing the Dalai Lama in the Potala palace, the Manchus tore down the Lhasa city walls and established a Qing protectorate over Tibet, but in 1723 they withdrew their military garrison from Lhasa, and a grandson of Güüshi Khan led an armed attempt to overthrow the Qing protectorate. Among the strongest supporters of the revolt were the heads of the Kumbum monastery. When the Manchus reestablished their control in Amdo in 1724 General Nian Gengyao showed the Kumbum lamas no mercy. At the monastery's entrance are eight stupas believed to contain the ashes of Kumbum's eight incarnate lamas at the time of the revolt. The Qing created a new territory named Qinghai, putting the Amdo tribal areas under the direct jurisdiction of the controller-general of Xining and assigning the urban and agricultural region of northeastern Amdo to Gansu province as Xining prefecture. The Manchus put most of the eastern Tibetan province of Kham under the administration of the Chinese province of Sichuan.

Upheavals in Tibetan politics led to Qing military expeditions to Lhasa again in 1728, 1750, and 1792 (to expel the Nepalese), and in 1772–1776 Qing armies conquered the inaccessible east Tibetan areas of mountainous rGyal-rong, known in Chinese as Jinchuan ("Gold River"). These campaigns, especially those in rGyal-rong, were immensely expensive, but they deepened the Qing emperor's paramount authority in Tibetan eyes. In the 1750s the Manchus had succeeded in destroying the Zunghars and had gone on from there to conquer Eastern Turkestan. The Qing government incorporated these two regions into the empire as a territory called Xinjiang, meaning "New Dominion."

Throughout the 18th century and during most of the 19th the Qing government maintained a moderately well enforced policy of isolating China proper from the empire's Inner Asian territories (Jilin and Heilongjiang in Manchuria, Inner and Outer Mongolia, Xinjiang, and the various regions of Tibet) because the dynasty still thought of itself as Manchu and wanted to preserve Inner Asia as a base for Qing control of China. Han immigration into Inner Asia was officially forbidden, except for a few designated areas. But the incorporation of the Manchurian frontier region, Mongolia, Xinjiang, and Tibet, together with China proper, inside a single, essentially Chinese empire opened Chinese Inner Asia to Han commercial enterprise as it had never been opened before. Chinese and Inner Asian economies grew increasingly intertwined. Inner Asians, particularly in Mongolia, piled up growing debts with Han trading houses. With time, more and more aspects of Han civilization made themselves felt in Inner Asia, and the Han language came into increasing use beyond the confines of China proper. Under the Qing dynasty a greater China gradually came into being, comprising the old "Middle Kingdom" of the Hans and most of the formerly non-Chinese realms along its landward bounds.

Population pressure and Russian expansion also eroded the Qing government's policy of closing Inner Asia to Han immigration. The Han population dramatically expanded in the 18th century—it seems roughly to have doubled—and it was impossible for the government to prevent some of this increase from making its way into Inner Asia. Shortly after the middle of the 19th century the Russians took advantage of Qing weaknesses, resulting mainly from the Taiping and other rebellions, and annexed all of China's northern and eastern Manchurian territories as well as a substantial amount of land along the Xinjiang border. To prevent further losses, the Qing government eventually reversed its policy and actively encouraged Han colonization of the sensitive borderlands.

In all of Qing Inner Asia, Han influences were least felt in Tibet proper (the Xizang Autonomous Region of today). In the late 1700s and in the 1800s, when the British in India made overtures to the Dalai Lama's government in Lhasa, hoping to obtain trade with Tibet and access to overland routes for commerce with China proper, the Lhasa authorities hid behind the Manchu emperor's protection and refused to negotiate with the British. Because Qing control over Tibet was too weak for the Qing government to be able to make any international agreements that would depend on Tibetan willingness to comply, the Lhasa government managed to keep the country isolated from external—principally British—political and commercial penetration throughout the 19th century.

In northeastern Tibet, on the other hand, Qing authority and power were real. In the 18th century, at Nian Gengyao's suggestion, the Manchus had decided to encourage the migration of Han colonists into Qinghai in order to strengthen the empire's presence among the unruly Amdo tribes despite the official Qing policy of segregating Inner Asia from China proper. Many Hans settled in the northeastern part of the territory, which became a base of imperial strength.

Contemporaneous with Han immigration into Qinghai was an acceleration in the diffusion of Islam in the same region. Growing numbers of Tibetans and Hans embraced the religion in the 18th and early 19th centuries as a result of Muslim missionary activities based in Shaanxi and Gansu. Some Muslim converts were farmers, but Muslims were more noticeable in commerce, transport, and military service.

In the 1860s, following the outbreak of the Taiping, Nian, and other rebellions against Qing rule in China proper and a major Muslim-dominated revolt in Yunnan that occurred simultaneously with a series of upheavals in Xinjiang, the Huis of Shaanxi, Gansu, and Qinghai provinces also went into revolt. Xinjiang followed suit, and an adventurer from western Central Asia named Ya'qūb Beg attempted to establish an independent emirate there. In the 1870s the Qing government reestablished its control over the entire Muslim northwest, with the exception of certain parts of Xinjiang, from which the Russians, who had occupied that territory's northwestern quarter during the rebellion, refused to withdraw. Having recovered the rest of Xinjiang, the Qing converted it into a

Chinese province. In northwest China proper the government resettled the Muslim population so as to separate Huis from Hans. In general, the authorities excluded Huis from living within the walls of cities but permitted them to reside in the suburbs. This segregation continued down to Wulsin's time and beyond.

The cultural position of Islam nevertheless remained strong in Gansu and Qinghai. In pastoral areas, inhabited by nomadic Tibetans and Mongols, Tibetan Buddhism remained dominant. The Gansu-Qinghai frontier area became an interface between the nomadic Buddhist and urban Muslim worlds. Animosities between Hans and Huis persisted, but apart from a major Muslim revolt centering on Xining and Xunhua in 1895–1896, Qinghai remained relatively stable and quiet for the rest of the Qing period.

In Tibet proper, in the late 19th century and early 20th when the British estimate of the Qing empire's strength was low, Anglo-Russian rivalry led to a British invasion and the taking of Lhasa in 1904. The British negotiated with the Lhasa government directly and concluded the 1904 Lhasa convention, which ignored the Qing empire's protectorate over Tibet. Then, in 1906, without consulting the Tibetans, the British signed a convention with the Qing in which Britain acknowledged that the Qing empire

was not a foreign power in Tibet and that the Qing were responsible for preserving Tibet's political integrity. In an Anglo-Russian convention of 1907 the British government further recognized "the suzerain rights of China" (meaning the Qing empire) in Tibet.

With international implications thus eliminated, the Qing sent an army into Tibet under General Zhao Erfeng, who subjected Kham to Qing control and then dispatched an expedition to Lhasa, which it entered early in 1910. The Dalai Lama fled to India, where he declared the Qing protectorate null and void, arguing that the invasion had violated the original relationship between the Dalai Lamas and the Manchu emperors. Zhao meanwhile drafted plans to annex all of southeast Tibet to China proper by creating a new province named Xikang, the western border of which would have reached within almost sixty miles of Lhasa. But before he could translate these plans into action, the Chinese revolution of 1911 erupted, and the Qing dynasty fell.

Most Hans eventually cut their queues and allowed the hair on their foreheads to grow, thus casting aside the hairstyle and dress that had symbolized their subjection to the Manchu ruling house. But in the Inner Asian borderlands, as Wulsin's pictures still show in 1923, the Manchu dress and hairstyle continued to predominate despite the dynasty's fall.

The Mê family [who lived] inside the Wall. The headdress is typical of that worn by the women of Wang Yeh Fu. Inner Mongolia.

The Regent of Alashan [right] younger brother of the king in the courtyard of his summer house. The king lives in Peking and the regent stays in Wang Yeh Fu by royal command. He is half Mongol and half Manchu and he speaks both Mongol and Chinese. He is intelligent, somewhat travelled and stuck off in this hole with nothing to do and scarcely the shadow of power.

In reality the power lies with the nearest Chinese garrison for the Mongols of the present day are too poorly armed and too few in number to oppose the Chinese with success. Inner Mongolia.

F.R.W. May 1923

The Early Republic and the Northwest Frontier

The dynasty's instrument of abdication was signed in 1912, investing Yuan Shikai, first president of the newly created republic, with authority over the Qing empire's "five peoples"—Manchus, Hans, Mongols, Muslims, and Tibetans—"together with their territory in its integrity" to form "one Great Republic of China." Yuan issued a proclamation that Mongolia, Xinjiang, and Tibet were henceforth considered to be on the same basis as provinces of the Republic of China. The Republic adopted a new Chinese flag consisting of five horizontal bars, each representing one of China's "five peoples": red, at the top, for the Hans, yellow for the Manchus, blue for the Mongols, white for the Muslims, and black for the Tibetans.

This classification reflected the territorial divisions of the former Qing empire but by no means did justice to China's ethnological composition. Concerned principally with territory, it emphasized spatially extensive but thinly populated Inner Asia and ignored the far more numerous peoples of the Chinese southwest Mention of the Manchus—by 1912 a numerically insignificant and almost totally sinicized people—brought in the provinces of Fengtian, Jilin, and Heilongjiang. Mention of the Muslims brought Xinjiang, but at the same time it had the effect of giving official ethnic status to a purely religious category, namely those who believed in Islam, underscoring the distinction between Hans and Chinese-speaking Huis. Assimilationist political leaders like Sun Yixian (Sun Yat-sen) tried to undo this by using the term "Tatar" instead of Hui when speaking of China's "five peoples," thus taking account of Xinjiang's Turkic-speaking population but leaving the door open for reclassification of the Chinese-speaking Huis as Hans.

During World War I (1914–1918) Muslim agents tried to win active support for a German-sponsored pan-Islamism among the Huis of China proper and among the Turkic-speaking peoples of Xinjiang. The Huis did not respond. Neither did Xinjiang's Turkic-speaking peoples, who were just then beginning their search for a new ethnolinguistic identity as Turks.

Having previously had no common name for themselves, Xinjiang's indigenous settled Turkic-speaking population finally chose the name of the Uighurs (now spelled Uygur in the official transcription system), who had conquered most of their region in the 8th century A.D. Significantly, the Uighurs' adoption of their name was initiated in 1921 not in Xinjiang but at a conference in Tashkent, in Soviet territory.

In the two Yellow Church countries, Tibet and Mongolia, separatist thinking was already widespread. Subordination to a supranational emperor was one thing, but subjection to what Tibetans and Mongols saw as a Han Chinese republic was quite another. They had been subjects of the Manchu emperors, the Tibetans and Mongols reasoned, not subjects of China, inasmuch as China, like Tibet and Mongolia, had merely been one of the Manchus' conquered territories. At the time of the dynasty's collapse the Dalai Lama was already in India declaring the Qing protectorate at an end, and in 1911 the Khalkha princes took a similar step, enthroning as their ruler the Jebtsundamba Khutughtu, the incarnate lama who headed the Outer Mongolian Yellow Church. The Russian government, to whom the Khalkhas looked for support, hesitated to back their claims to full independence, but in 1912 Russia officially pledged to help maintain Outer Mongolia's "autonomous regime."

At the beginning of 1913 Tibetan and Outer Mongolian representatives signed a treaty at Urga (now Ulan Bator, capital of the MPR) declaring their independence of China and agreeing to strengthen Tibeto-Mongolian ties. A month later, the Dalai Lama formally declared Tibetan independence at Lhasa while his troops expelled from western Kham the remaining military forces of the Republic of China, driving them beyond the Mekong-Salween divide. Later that year Russia and China jointly declared Outer Mongolia to be autonomous under Chinese suzerainty and undertook not to interfere in the country's internal affairs, not to send armed forces there, and not to colonize. In 1915 a tripartite agreement between Russia,

China, and Outer Mongolia confirmed the 1913 joint declaration and admitted Outer Mongolia's right to make commercial agreements with other states.

The Republic of China's government at Beijing never relinquished its claims to Tibet, and it agreed reluctantly to Outer Mongolia's autonomy only because of pressure from Russia, from Japanese encroachment in north China, and because of its own internal weaknesses. But in 1917 the Russian revolution temporarily neutralized Russia as an international power; so Chinese troops under Xu Shuzheng invaded Outer Mongolia in 1919 and cancelled its autonomy. This act turned Outer Mongolian opinion strongly against China. In 1921 Russian counterrevolutionary troops, reinforced by anti-Chinese Mongolian volunteers and with the indirect backing of Japan, occupied Urga, but their behavior won them few friends, and Outer Mongolian sentiment switched to the side of the Russian Red Army, which entered the country at the request of Mongolian revolutionaries, drove out the Russian counterrevolutionaries, and established an independent Mongolian People's Revolutionary Government.

Separatist feelings also existed in some quarters in Inner Mongolia, Gansu, and Qinghai, but Chinese

power was greater there and nearer at hand. The Beijing-Suiyuan Railway, which had already reached Kalgan (Zhangjiakou) by 1909, drawing that part of Inner Mongolia more tightly to China, was being extended westward, gradually opening the region to Han colonization and facilitating Chinese military transport.

Yet China's political integration was ebbing away. During the presidency of strongman Yuan Shikai, the central government had maintained its authority by confirming *de facto* military leaders in the provinces as autonomous military governors. After Yuan's death in 1916 even the semblances of centralized rule began to dissolve, and the military governors transformed themselves into semi-independent warlords. Each of these, while paying lip service to China's unity, hoped at the least to prolong his personal autonomy indefinitely. A few aspired to more than regional power and hoped to reunite the country under their own command.

In western Inner Mongolia (which later became Ningxia), Gansu, and Qinghai, control lay mainly in the grip of a number of Hui military officers, who acted in the name of the Republic of China. The Han presence, especially in Qinghai, was little felt.

The Great Golden Stupa of Labrang, Gansu.

Wulsin's Time:
Inner Mongolia, Gansu, and Qinghai in 1923

When Wulsin and his companions traversed the northwest frontier in 1923, all China was tense, north and south, but in the south armies were on the move as warlords and nationalist revolutionaries struggled with one another for power. Wulsin had chosen Gansu as his destination, "where everything is quiet." But the momentary quiet carried no assurance of protection along the way. Bandits often attacked Inner Mongolian settlements and robbed caravans, which had to proceed under armed escort, their safety being "guaranteed for ½ dollar per camel." On Wulsin's route there were reports of a recent fight with 200 brigands, and shortly before Wulsin reached Yitiaoshan, on the west bank of the Yellow River just south of the Great Wall, brigands had made a bloody attack on the salt administration warehouse there.

Inner Mongolia in 1923 was on the eve of a great surge of Han colonists into the region. That year the Beijing-Suiyuan Railway reached Baotou, the starting point of Wulsin's trek—Wulsin himself arrived on it—and telegraph and telephone services were already in operation.

At Baotou the jurisdiction of the central Beijing government was a reality, but the government was caught up in the warlord factional struggles of the Zhili clique, and military control rested with a Muslim general, Ma Fuxiang, whose family had been noteworthy in its loyalty to the Qing dynasty during the Muslim rebellions of the 19th century. In 1912 Ma had transferred his loyalty to the Republic, which he had served in various military capacities in western Inner Mongolia, Gansu, and Qinghai. At the beginning of 1921, after seven years as guards commander of the Ningxia (now Yinchuan) district, Ma had taken up his new post at Guisui (now Hohhot) as military governor of the Inner Mongolian special district of Suiyuan, where Wulsin met him and was given cards of introduction to Ma's nephew in Ningxia and to his kinsman Ma Qi, the military commander at Xining.

Despite the Suiyuan governor's identification with the Beijing government, Wulsin noted that Han-Hui animosities were not dead. Beijing, Wulsin said, had imposed Han soldiers from Zhili and Shandong on Ma Fuxiang, and these fought with his Gansu Hui soldiers whenever the two were together.

Farther to the southwest, in Qinghai and along the southern Gansu-Qinghai border, Hui military dominance was virtually complete. The Huis, Wulsin observed, "are in practical control of the whole frontier from Sining [Xining] through Hochow [Hezhou, now Linxia] to T'aochow [Taozhou]. This is their stronghold, though other Mohammedan settlements are found in Ninghsia [Ningxia], far away to the north east, and in Chang chia ch'uan [Zhangjiachuan] in the east."

Of Ma Qi, the Hui commander at Xining who supplied the expedition with a Muslim interpreter and two Muslim soldiers for its travels in Qinghai, Wulsin wrote, "His forces are the sturdiest and readiest to fight on the whole border." Some time before Wulsin's trip the monks at Labrang had "almost murdered a [Christian] missionary who tried to photograph the temple." In 1921, defying Xining, the Labrang monks had "gathered an army of [Tibetan] tribesmen." But "in a battle close to the monastery they were thoroughly beaten by . . . [Ma Qi's] trained Moslem soldiers." Having administered this "thrashing" to the Labrang monks, forcing them to tolerate the presence of Christian missionaries, Ma Qi quartered a 300-man Muslim battalion in the Labrang village and was further reinforcing this at the time of Wulsin's visit. Wulsin recorded that "a Mohammedan official [at Labrang] made the lamas keep quiet while we photographed the great chanting hall, and forced an entrance for us to the museum." Wulsin's guide at Labrang was a Muslim, "a great bearded veteran of the Mohammedan rebellion, long exiled among the Tibetans, and now supremely powerful over their fate in the Labrang region, because of his post as official interpreter at the yamen [government office] in the town."

Ma Qi had also run into difficulties in 1921 with the Tibetan mGo-log tribesmen. "One of the General's agents was killed by the Goloks" [mGo-log] who lived in the bend of the Yellow River south of Lake Kokonor, where "it seems that gold is worked." In reprisal Ma Qi "sent an expedition which almost annihilated one of the three Golok tribes." By 1923 Ma Qi had "brought the Kokonor region to heel" as far west as the Tsaidam, and, according to Wulsin, his power extended "beyond Jyekundo [sKye-rgu-mdo, now Yushu in southern Qinghai]; I believe beyond Chamdo [Chab-mdo, now Changdu at the eastern end of the Xizang Autonomous Region], but not very much further." (The second assertion is most unlikely.) Wulsin, whose interests lay with the protection of foreigners, saw Ma Qi as "in many ways a public benefactor. He has brought peace all along the border."

The Tibetans, of course, were offended by Ma Qi's protection of foreign missionaries among their holiest Buddhist shrines, disliked Muslim domination, and, not least, resented the taxation that Ma Qi imposed on the Tibetan population, nomad and sedentary

alike. "People say," as Wulsin puts it in his journal, "that the Tibetans have it in for Ma Ch'i [Ma Qi] and his men, because of the heavy taxes he levies, and that when next the Moslems have trouble with China a Tibetan army will strike them in the back."

Wulsin's overall impression of the Gansu-Qinghai frontier was a hopeful one, apart from the region's underlying political tensions. "Supplying food in Kansu [Gansu] is easy;" he wrote, "the province furnishes meat, vegetables and fruit in abundance." But he also noted, "Kansu is a funny province in that way; rich and poor regions lie side by side." There were frequent evidences of earlier destruction, still unrepaired. Signs of the 19th-century Muslim rebellions were still visible, as were ruins from the 1920 earthquake, and from other disasters, such as the depredations of the White Wolf outlaws at Taozhou as far back as 1914. "There are still ruins to be seen inside the [Taozhou Old City] walls," he wrote in his journal, and at Taozhou New City he and his companions again "saw a few ruins left by White Wolf." Nevertheless, Wulsin and his party went unmolested, suffering few inconveniences and no privations along their way.

The morning market at the Labrang Lamasery, Gansu.

Since Then

After 1923 numerous events changed the face of Chinese Inner Asia. In Outer Mongolia, following the Jebtsundamba Khutughtu's death in 1924, the revolutionaries established the Mongolian People's Republic (MPR) and, with Soviet support, kept their country separate from China while they carried through a radical program of social revolution and modernization. The central and western regions of Tibet, under the Dalai Lama's government in Lhasa, also stayed beyond the Republic of China's control.

Inner Mongolia

Relations between Mongols and Hans in Inner Mongolia had been deteriorating since the final decade of the 19th century. The root cause was Han colonization, which had been steadily increasing, and which limited the nomads' pastoral movements and reduced their pasture. The growing Han presence and indebtedness to Han merchants at a time when the Mongols were becoming increasingly aware of themselves as a people with a common history and culture encouraged separatist inclinations among ordinary rank-and-file Mongols.

Among the princes, however, fear of the MPR's revolutionary influence was growing. The threat of revolution and possible Soviet domination prompted the Inner Mongolian princes to cling to China and so to encourage Han settlement in their domains. By 1923 many refugees from Russia had passed through Inner Mongolia, and the social objectives of the October revolution were comparatively well known. Wulsin, after traveling through Ningxia, noted in his journal, "Here and there we found Russian inscriptions on the walls, written by refugees. The same refugees must have tasted much bitterness, for many of them fled clear across Turkestan and China without a cent to their names." For princes and lamas, inclusion in the Soviet-protected MPR would have meant the loss of princely and monastic privileges.

Some princes and lamas and many of the commoners and lesser nobility were nonetheless attracted to separatist ideas and to moderate programs for social change. By the end of 1925 two political parties favoring Inner Mongolian autonomy and social reform had taken shape. One party was the Young Mongols, whose main leader was Prince Demchügdonggrub, known for short as De Wang (Prince De). The Young Mongols advocated modification of princely privileges and desired Inner Mongolian autonomy within the Republic of China's political system. The other party was the Inner Mongolian People's Revolutionary Party (IMPRP), headed by a partially sinicized Mongol named Buyantai, who espoused the China-oriented revolutionism of the Guomindang. The IMPRP wanted to replace the rule of the princes with a more representative democratic structure and advocated political autonomy within a federated Republic of China based on Sun Yixian's *Three People's Principles.* At this time the Guomindang was allied with the Chinese Communists and the USSR and was on cordial—although not fully defined—terms with the MPR; so the IMPRP also desired a close relationship with the MPR.

The IMPRP sent several young Inner Mongols to study in the MPR and at Sun Yixian University in Moscow. Among these was a sinicized (he did not speak Mongolian) Tümed Mongol named Yunze, who became a Communist in 1927 and adopted the revolutionary name Ulanfu (meaning, partly in Mongolian and partly in Chinese, the Red One).

When Jiang Jieshi (Chiang Kai-shek) broke with the USSR and the Chinese Communists in 1926, captured Beijing (renaming it Beiping—its old name from the early Ming dynasty), and in 1928 established a right-wing Guomindang government at Nanjing, Buyantai terminated the IMPRP's relations with the MPR and merged his party with Jiang Jieshi's Guomindang. But in 1928 the Nanjing government abolished Inner Mongolia, creating four Chinese provinces—Rehe, Chahar, Suiyuan, and Ningxia. The Inner Mongols felt that Buyantai had betrayed them; so he and his IMPRP lost all effectiveness. This left De Wang's Young Mongols as the only indigenous mobilizers of Inner Mongolian national sentiment.

45

To allay the anxieties of the princes and lamas, the Nanjing government accorded them greater powers than ever, guaranteeing their authority with Chinese military forces. But the military forces also guaranteed the safety of Han immigrants, who came in increasing numbers to colonize what had formerly been Mongolian pastures.

In 1931 the Japanese invaded the three eastern provinces of Liaoning (formerly called Fengtian), Jilin, and Heilongjiang and in 1932 declared them independent of China under the name Manzhouguo. In 1933 Manzhouguo annexed Rehe province—a region of what had formerly been Inner Mongolia—and created an autonomous Mongolian province, named Xingan, out of the Mongolian areas of the former Rehe, Liaoning, and Heilongjiang, banning all Han settlement in the new province. This gained an important propaganda advantage for the Japanese against the Republic of China in Inner Mongolia.

Nostalgia for the Qing empire was also a potent undercurrent among the Inner Mongols, who had always regarded themselves not as a conquered people (like the Hans) but as the Manchus' dynastic allies. The Japanese, who were not insensitive to such sentiments, formally reestablished the Qing dynasty in 1934, enthroning Puyi, the last Qing scion, as the Manzhouguo emperor. Under the watchful eyes of Japanese "advisers" the Mongolian princes of Xingan could continue to rule their subjects, dreaming that they were still living in the great days of the Qing.

While Ulanfu and his colleagues worked to arouse revolutionary consciousness and anti-Japanese sentiment in Inner Mongolia, De Wang and his followers convened a conference in 1933 to form a western Inner Mongolian government (the eastern Inner Mongols being those in Manzhouguo) and to demand greater autonomy from the Republic of China. The Nanjing government gave some token concessions but obstructed all attempts to make Inner Mongolian autonomy a reality. Despairing of winning anything from the Guomindang, De Wang formed an Inner Mongolian government in 1936 with secret Japanese aid. This created a split within the Mongolian leadership. A China-oriented coalition withdrew from De Wang's nationalist movement, but De Wang held his ground and joined Manzhouguo in an unsuccessful attempt to invade Suiyuan.

The next year, 1937, Jiang Jieshi and the Chinese

Communists re-cemented their former alliance, creating a united front against the Japanese, and Ulanfu reemerged in Inner Mongolia as a political commissar. But with the outbreak of the Sino-Japanese War in July, the Japanese army, supported by De Wang's cavalry, overran Suiyuan and established a Mongolian Federated Autonomous Government. Meanwhile Ulanfu escaped to the Chinese Communists' wartime capital at Yanan, where he began to help in the formation of the Communists' national minority policies. In November 1938 the Communist leader Mao Zedong gave a speech in which he promised Mongols, Muslims ("Hui"), Miaos, and Tibetans ("Fan") equal rights with Hans, plus autonomy within a unified Chinese state. But unlike earlier policy statements, the speech did not offer them the right to secede.

De Wang and his Inner Mongolian nationalists suffered disappointments from the Japanese occupation akin to those that they had suffered from the Guomindang. The Japanese kept De Wang's western Inner Mongols separate from the eastern Inner Mongols of Manzhouguo and in 1940 even reaffirmed the western Inner Mongols' subordination to China by placing them under Japan's puppet Chinese government at Nanjing.

When Japan's military forces began to collapse, De Wang's nationalists tried to forestall the danger of being considered Japanese collaborators by coordinating their efforts in 1945 to expel the Japanese activists before Japan's defeat. At the encouragement of the vice-president of the MPR, the Inner Mongolian nationalists created a provisional government, but later that year the Communist Eighth Route Army entered Inner Mongolia, disbanded the provisional government, and replaced it with the more revolutionary Inner Mongolian Autonomy Movement Association (IMAMA) under Ulanfu.

The USSR had annexed Uriyangkhai, formerly a territory of Qing Outer Mongolia, in 1944, and a plebiscite officially sanctioned the MPR's total separation from China in 1945. The Republic of China's Guomindang government, now a USSR ally, recognized the MPR's independence in 1946.

In Inner Mongolia the situation remained fluid. Nationalist followers of De Wang, pro-Guomindang followers of Buyantai, a rival China-oriented faction known as the Suiyuan group, and another coalition representing the interests of the nobility vied with one another for power. All these groups were composed of people who wanted, in one form or another, an autonomous Inner Mongolia that would comprise all of China's Mongolian areas, from Ningxia to Heilongjiang. The Guomindang leadership opposed the formation of such a united autonomous entity. The Communists, on the other hand, favored it. The result was that in April 1947 Ulanfu's IMAMA was able to unite sympathizers from most of the eastern and western Inner Mongolian districts to form a People's Government for what has now become the Nei Monggol (Inner Mongolian) Autonomous Region (NMAR).

The last holdout was Alashan. De Wang, who had escaped to Chongqing after the Japanese collapse in 1945, moved to Beiping and lived there under the watch of the Guomindang until 1948, shortly before the Communists occupied Beiping (renaming it Beijing). Then De Wang suddenly flew to Alashan and joined forces with Darijaya, the Alashan prince. Darijaya, being one of the richest and most powerful princes of Inner Mongolia, represented princely privilege in a way that De Wang, who had cut off his queue and asked his princely colleagues to forego their privileges, did not. The residents of Dingyuanying (Wulsin's Wangyefu), supported Darijaya, but the village Mongols disliked him. They were, however, afraid to oppose him openly, because he had dealt severely with those who had shown democratic inclinations.

Under the circumstances many right-wing Mongols joined the De Wang/Darijaya alliance and formed an anti-Communist government, but the alliance lacked a wide enough appeal to challenge the People's Government of the NMAR. In a last-ditch effort to win over the Inner Mongols, the Guomindang recognized the Alashan government as an autonomous province within the Republic of China, but by then it was September 1949. Later that month Communist-allied military forces from Suiyuan put an end to the Alashan venture, and the Communists incorporated Alashan into the NMAR.

Since 1949 the Han population has continued to grow, and the Inner Mongols have been increasingly involved in China's political, cultural, and economic life—especially at Baotou, where Wulsin began his trip. Here, in a zone where both Hans and Mongols have farmed since at least the time of Altan Khan in

the 16th century, spring wheat and other crops are grown; sugar is produced; and Baotou has become a major industrial district, drawing on nearby deposits of coal to fuel its production of iron, steel, and aluminum. Old nomadic methods of animal husbandry are giving way to new techniques. Schools and medical facilities are being introduced. A Latin alphabetic transcription system (*pinyin*), based on the official transcription system for the Han Chinese language, has been devised for Mongolian.

The PRC government has varied in the degree to which it has tried to preserve the distinctiveness of Mongolian culture, but in matters of territory the realities of the Han population growth could not but be taken into account. In the 1960s the NMAR comprised essentially all the Inner Mongolian districts of the old Qing empire. Now, however, its political boundaries have been redrawn, and it is reduced once again to roughly those territories that Inner Mongolia covered in the early years of the Republic of China, between 1912 and 1928.

Muslim and Tibetan Regions

In the 1920s Muslim politics dominated Inner Mongolia's Ningxia region, Gansu, Qinghai, and Xinjiang. In the southern Gansu-Qinghai frontier area Hui officers held military power and represented the sovereignty of the Republic, but there was always the possibility that Hans, backed up by Chinese central authority, might wrest that power from them. More remote, but nonetheless present in Qinghai and eastern Kham, was another challenge to Hui dominance, a challenge that also repudiated Chinese sovereignty—namely the influence of Lhasa, neither fully secular nor merely religious, tacitly denying Chinese claims to Amdo, volubly denying them to Kham, and always reminding all Tibetans that Amdo and Kham were provinces of Tibet.

Wulsin's informants had predicted trouble between the Xining military commander Ma Qi and the Tibetans. The trouble soon came. In 1925 the Labrang incarnation withdrew from the monastery in protest against Ma Qi's heavy taxes. Wool and hides merchants followed suit. The busy commerce of the Labrang village slackened, drying up the duties on trade that had formed an important part of Ma Qi's revenues. An army of Tibetan fighting men seized Labrang from Ma Qi's Hui forces, but Ma counter-

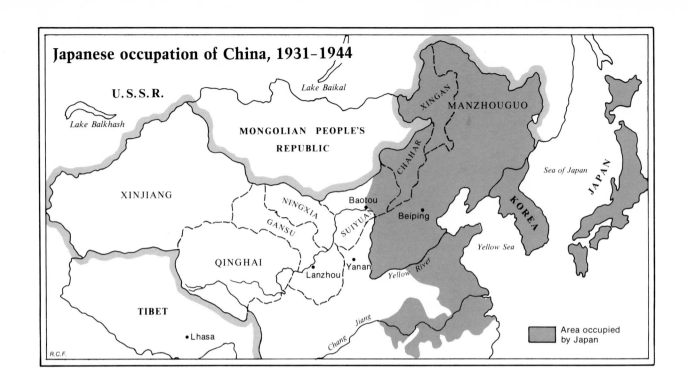

Japanese occupation of China, 1931–1944

U.S.S.R.

Lake Baikal

Lake Balkhash

MONGOLIAN PEOPLE'S
REPUBLIC

XINGAN

MANZHOUGUO

CHAHAR

XINJIANG

NINGXIA

Baotou

GANSU

SUIYUAN

Beiping

Sea of Japan

JAPAN

KOREA

QINGHAI

Lanzhou

Yanan

Yellow Sea

Yellow River

TIBET

•Lhasa

Chang Jiang

R.C.F.

Area occupied
by Japan

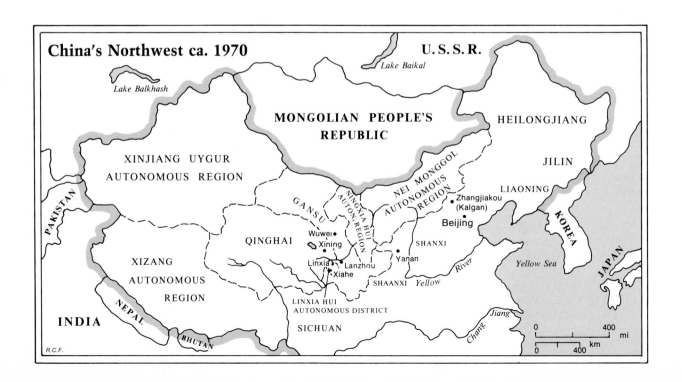

China's Northwest ca. 1970

U.S.S.R.

Lake Baikal

Lake Balkhash

MONGOLIAN PEOPLE'S
REPUBLIC

HEILONGJIANG

XINJIANG UYGUR
AUTONOMOUS REGION

JILIN

PAKISTAN

GANSU

NINGXIA HUI
AUTON. REGION

NEI MONGGOL
AUTONOMOUS
REGION

LIAONING

Zhangjiakou
(Kalgan)

QINGHAI

Wuwei•

Xining

Beijing

KOREA

XIZANG

Linxia

Lanzhou

SHANXI

Yanan

•Xiahe

Yellow Sea

JAPAN

AUTONOMOUS

SHAANXI

Yellow

River

REGION

INDIA

NEPAL

LINXIA HUI
AUTONOMOUS DISTRICT

Chang

Jiang

BHUTAN

SICHUAN

0   400
mi

0   400
km

R.C.F.

attacked violently, slaughtering great numbers of Tibetans, and thus reestablished his control.

Later that year army units of the powerful Han warlord Feng Yuxiang entered Gansu, posing a new threat to Hui authority. Feng's subordinate Liu Yufen was made Gansu governor, and in 1926 he took action to reduce the Huis to obedience. Feng's taxation and conscription policies especially outraged Hui opinion; so in 1928 an underlying current of Muslim rebellion broke through the surface at Liangzhou (now Wuwei) in the Gansu corridor, and the rebellion soon spread into the southern part of the province, including Xining and Ma Qi's south Gansu-Qinghai frontier.

It was at just this time, in 1928, that the Republic of China's government reorganized its provincial structure, carving up Inner Mongolia into four provinces. In Qinghai, the Nationalist government formalized the existing power structure in 1928 by designating Qinghai as a province and by detaching Xining prefecture from its nominal subordination to Gansu, making Xining the Qinghai capital and naming Ma Qi as governor. Labrang and its environs, being under Ma Qi's *de facto* control, were officially designated as Xiahe district and attached to Qinghai. (Xiahe's territory has subsequently been reassigned to Gansu.)

Because Chinese military forces were still occupying the eastern part of the Tibetan province of Kham, the Republic also proclaimed a province there in 1928 called Xikang, but it was far smaller than the one that Zhao Erfeng had planned in 1910. Xikang's western border remained in dispute. In practice the Tibet-Xikang frontier lay roughly along the Jinsha Jiang, which is the upper course of the Chang Jiang (Yangtze River), but down through the 1940s, even on the Chinese side of the river, the indigenous Tibetan population would not accept the Republic of China's currency.

Despite the Muslim rebellion in Gansu and Qinghai, the principal Hui military leaders of the two provinces maintained their allegiance to the Republic, but they chafed under Feng Yuxiang's domination. When Feng quarreled with Jiang Jieshi and declared his independence of the Nanjing government in 1929, the Muslim warlords saw their chance, repudiated Feng, and declared their allegiance to Nanjing. This eliminated Feng's power base in Gansu; so the Nationalist government saw the Gansu-Qinghai Hui *status quo*

as tested allies of Nanjing's authority in the northwest and augmented the Hui officers' power accordingly. Under these conditions the Muslim rebellion gradually subsided, ceasing altogether in 1931.

Soviet-trained Uzbeks and Kirghiz tried to rekindle Hui sentiments against China, but their efforts were unavailing. In 1931, acting on the Nationalists' orders, Ma Qi's son Ma Bufang drove a rival Hui leader, Ma Zhongying, who was thought to be a Soviet protégé, out of Gansu into Xinjiang, where Ma Zhongying aided his Muslim coreligionists in a revolt in 1931–1934. At first, Ma Zhongying was defeated and withdrew his Hui forces back to Gansu, but he returned to Xinjiang in 1933 and won many victories before a Han warlord, General Sheng Shicai, took over the Xinjiang government and, with Soviet help, forced Ma in 1934 to take refuge in the USSR.

Like his father before him, Ma Bufang maintained as tight a control as possible over the entire area of Qinghai, keeping the Tibetan and Mongolian tribes in line. In 1932 he joined forces with the governor of Sichuan to reassert Chinese authority in Xikang, where the Republic's garrison commander Ma Su had intervened in a Tibetan dispute, only to have Tibetan forces drive the Chinese east of the Yalong River. After pushing the Tibetans back to the Jinsha Jiang, Ma Bufang took advantage of his success to negotiate a Qinghai-Tibetan peace treaty. A Tibetan autonomy movement led to renewed fighting in Xikang in 1936. Xikang's provincial government was not inaugurated until 1939.

In 1934–1935 the Communists made their famous Long March through Xikang into eastern Gansu and Shaanxi. Although hoping to use the background of Han-Hui antagonism to win Muslim support against the Guomindang government, the Communists were sorely disappointed. The Huis, being an explicitly religious category rather than an ethnolinguistic group, felt themselves more threatened by the Communists' anti-religious position than by the Guomindang's assimilationism. Muslim military forces attacked the Communists as they approached, and in Gansu, Hui cavalry nearly annihilated some of the Long March units. To soften the Muslims' attitudes the Communists promised the Huis an autonomous government and offered to help them unify the Muslim peoples of China with the Muslims of the Mongolian People's Republic and the USSR.

Japan was another power that tried unsuccessfully to win the Huis away from their support of the Nanjing government. Japanese propaganda efforts had already achieved substantial results in Inner Mongolia. In the early 1930s Japan's propagandists had striven to arouse a Japan-sponsored pan-Islamism among the Huis, and in 1937 and 1938 the Japanese directly approached Ma Bufang, who was then the acting governor of Qinghai, but without result. Ma Hongkui, governor of Ningxia, also maintained a sharp watch against Japanese influence. In 1938 he sent his soldiers to Dingyuanying, captured the city, and took Prince Darijaya of Alashan into custody solely because a Japanese military officer had visited the prince earlier that year.

Throughout World War II China's Muslim and Tibetan areas stayed quiet. Hui military and administrative officials in Gansu and Qinghai kept up their allegiance to the Guomindang. In Tibet proper the Lhasa government pursued a policy of strict isolation, ignoring Chinese claims to sovereignty over Tibet and minimizing contact with Xikang. In the far northwest, Xinjiang continued to recognize the Chinese government's authority, but soon after Sheng Shicai's takeover in 1933 the province came under heavy Soviet influence, where it remained for a decade until the war against Germany diverted Soviet resources to Europe. In 1944 a revolt detached Xinjiang's Ili region and, with Soviet encouragement, proclaimed Ili's independence as the East Turkestan Republic. Ili remained independent until 1949, when it and the rest of Xinjiang voluntarily joined the Communist side and a Provisional People's Government was formed.

In Ningxia, Gansu, and Qinghai, Xinjiang's separatism elicited no response. Even in 1949, as the Guomindang forces disintegrated in China proper, most of the Hui leaders remained on the Guomindang side until the end. Ma Bufang and Ma Hongkui joined forces against the Communists in the northwest, and for a brief time Xining became the capital of the refugee Guomindang government.

Since 1949, quiet has reigned among the Huis of Ningxia, Gansu, and Qinghai, and in 1958 a Ningxia Hui Autonomous Region was inaugurated to satisfy Muslim aspirations. Originally the region consisted only of what had been the southeastern corner of the Republic's Ningxia province plus the former Guyuan

area of Gansu, but subsequently Ningxia's territory has been extended north, to the border of the MPR, thus underscoring the separation of the westernmost Inner Mongolian territories from the NMAR and the inclusion of those territories in the province of Gansu. An additional Muslim area is the Linxia Hui Autonomous District, containing the shrines of Hezhou (now Linxia), the "Chinese Mecca," on Gansu's Qinghai frontier.

Xinjiang has been less quiet. In 1955 the PRC created the Xinjiang Uygur (Uighur) Autonomous Region with an administrative structure designed to give adequate recognition to Xinjiang's diverse ethnic composition, but violent resistance to reforms erupted there in 1958–1959, followed by considerable emigration to the USSR. In 1962 there was a major revolt in Ili, and in 1967–1968 the excesses of the Cultural Revolution in Xinjiang triggered another revolt.

China's Tibetan areas have also witnessed some turbulence since 1949. In 1950 Communist forces, with the help of Khambas (people of Kham) who resented Xikang's separation from central Tibet, invaded Tibet proper and forced the Dalai Lama's government to sign an agreement in 1951 that Tibet was an integral part of China. The PRC retained Qinghai and Xikang as provinces and gave Tibet proper autonomy under the Dalai Lama. In 1955, however, the PRC government abolished Xikang, incorporating into Sichuan all the Tibetan territory east of the Jinsha Jiang and recognizing the territory west of it as belonging to the Lhasa government. But reforms in the new Sichuan territories provoked a Khamba revolt in 1956, after which many disgruntled Khambas fled to Lhasa, where they began encouraging resistance to the Communist cadres.

In Qinghai the PRC developed the Xining district's industrial potential (mainly textiles) and nearby sources of coal, linking northeastern Qinghai by rail with central China. Oil deposits in the Tsaidam added further value to the region. But Communist programs sparked abortive uprisings in the Tibetan areas of Qinghai and Gansu in 1958. Since then the Tibetan northeast has been calm.

Tibet's last revolt flared up in 1959. The Khamba refugees played an important role in mobilizing Tibetan opinion against the PRC, and partly from fear and partly as an act of resistance, the Dalai Lama fled to India. His absence from Lhasa only facilitated the

Communists' task of incorporating Tibet more fully into China. In 1962 Tibet was the scene of a Sino-Indian border war. The PRC inaugurated the Xizang Autonomous Region in 1965.

As in Inner Mongolia, so also in China's Muslim and Tibetan regions: Communist revolution has brought closer cultural, political, and economic ties with China proper and has increased the influence of Han civilization in non-Han borderlands. It has brought literacy, modern education, better medical facilities, and greater productive capacity. It has brought secular ideals of social equality and wider awareness of the world. But each of these gifts contains challenges to traditional ways of life. It remains to be seen how much of the distinctive character of China's non-Han peoples will survive the impact of her modernity.

The famous Lamasery of Kumbum, one of the most sacred temples in all Tibet, with its roofs of pure gold plate, its great figure of Tsong Kaba, the Buddhist saint and its 3000 lamas in their filthy robes of red and yellow and their everlasting smell of rancid butter. We were received by the living Buddha to whom we brought gifts, an Ingersoll Radiolite watch, a compass and some sugar. Qinghai.
J.W. August 1923

Photographs

The railroad from Peking to Paotow had been
completed to this point only a short time before and
is still running on temporary track, well ballasted
but layed along the ground.

Baotou Inner Mongolia

Paotow, this frontier town (on the border of Mongolia and near the Yellow River) of 150,000 inhabitants—the western terminus of the Peking Suiyuan Railroad is picturesque—mud walls and mud houses on the side of a treeless hill. There have been many festivals since we came and Mongols in their brilliant oranges and magentas and their big boots have filled the market places—carts of Chinese girls in bright red coats, well greased hair and feet smaller than I have ever seen have come from all the surrounding countryside. Stiltwalkers in fantastic costume have entertained us and small children dressed as fairies have come to sing for us in the evenings.

J.W. March 1923

Paotow is a booming town. The railroad has just reached there and warehouses and trading establishments are springing up on every side. The half-mile from the railroad track to the river was a bare brown plain in March 1923. In October of that same year one great mud-wall enclosure after another [had] sprung up in the interval to cover the empty space of 6 months before. The people of Paotow are [Han] Chinese, the big, northern Chinese who eat wheat and millet, are at home in a dry country, and do their work with horses, mules, and camels. They think of rice as an imported delicacy and in most cases view a boat with horrified apprehension.

F.R.W. October 1923

Entrance to a big trading house in Paotow. Loaded camels coming in from the desert. The tower in the center is of pierced brick; it is filled with coal and ignited to illuminate the night during the celebration of the festival in the first moon season.

Taxi stand.

Meat vendor's stall at the Paotow market.

Courtyard of a carpet factory in Paotow. Wool hung up ready for dyeing. In the right hand corner are great blocks of famous Shansi coal.

Two [Han] Chinese working on a flat stove attached by a pipe to a bellows.

Weighing lumps of coal. The coal of Shansi commonly used in the Paotow region is of beautiful quality and is transported in huge lumps 2 feet across.

Crowd at an outdoor theatrical performance during the festival at the beginning of the second moon. The big building is the stage. Spectators use their carts for boxes.

[*Han*] *Stilt dancers in the streets of Paotow.*

[Han] Stilt dancers in fantastic costumes dancing in inn courtyard at Paotow.

Alashan Inner Mongolia

Ch'ang Fan Ch'uan trading post. The owner of the trading post buys what the Mongols produce, skins, wool, animals, etc. and in return sells them anything they require: in his long dark storeroom we saw boots, iron tent pegs, braziers for dung fires, horseshoes, ladles, great pots for tea, cloth, baskets, sacks, sweetmeats, matches. The compound is a huge one 225 ft. x 150 ft. The main courtyard is big and so are the houses which open onto it; and all around the enclosure lies another great series of courtyards to accommodate the livestock of the trading post and the animals of visiting Mongols. The whole post is built of dried mud with high outer walls, flat topped roofs whose parapets are loopholed here and there and a great massive gate that would do honor to a fortress. The walls support the roof, not vertical timbers as in the typical [Han] Chinese house. Here and there the walls are reinforced with great piers built of round boulders. One comes through the gateway into a forecourt empty except for piles of brushwood fuel and the tracks of many goats. Beyond is a sharp turn and then the main court big enough for fifty camels with buildings on three sides of it. On one side is a flour mill worked by two donkeys; on the other a series of rooms. In the center is the main house where the trader and his men seem to live: two big dirt floored rooms with k'angs [a bed built of brick or earth so that it can be heated with a fire underneath] to accommodate an army, and stoves where cooking goes on at all hours. There is a polished table where sedate games of dominoes are played with a tall stack of bright copper cash in front of each player. By day the whole place is in twilight except near the door; at night wicks floating in oil in tall iron lamps light it up shifting the shadows to new places and bringing out the fine polish of old black wood counters and chests. Outside the yellow grass and the sand dunes begin.

F.R.W. April 1923

Mongol soldiers, picturesque and tough looking wore a mixture of native and foreign dress with characters on the breast and bath towel turbans. They carried [Han] Chinese army rifles (the early German Mauser model) and in some cases native knives. They rode Mongol ponies with Chinese saddles. Their reputation is good. They are said to be hard fighters, dreaded by the bandits, but orderly and honest in their dealings with civilians. They belong to the army of the king of Alashan and guard the roads (and collect taxes).

F. R. W.   April 1923

Tze Wanze Jing. No longer a trading post, it is now headquarters for 22 Mongol soldiers who patrol the road. They have set up a typical Mongol tent in the middle of the courtyard.

Traders at Tung Pi Fang, a farm trading post.

The country (just north of the great bend of the Yellow River) keeps changing; sometimes it is flat and again it becomes rolling; long yellow grass appears where there is moisture and shorter brown tufts where there is not. There are isolated farms all through the region. [Han] Chinese settlers are taking up the land wherever irrigation is possible and they are pressing the Mongols back into a country so arid that it can only be used for grazing. There are a few Mongols along the route living in their round felt tents and caring for their flocks. Camel caravans for Kansu and Turkestan constantly traverse [this area]. At certain seasons of the year there is a good deal of water in the ground and marshy places are not infrequent. This is a true frontier, with all the excitement, the optimism, the empty spaces, and the occasional disorders which the word suggests.

F. R. W.   April 1923

A Mongol Family.

Mongols at a desert well.

Pastoral Mongols. [Their] tents are little round buildings of felt stretched on a wooden framework, warm snug houses for the bitter cold winter, which can be taken down or set up in a few hours. They feed and follow the cattle, horses, sheep and goats, eat the flesh, drink the milk, sell the hair and wool. All their wealth is in animals and their lives are governed accordingly. We think of pasture as green, rich, and waving. Here it is sparse and dry, the grass growing in tufts. The dry stony country, like a level brown floor with patches of grass gives place to a desert of sand and dry brush that rose and fell in dunes and hillocks.

F. R. W.   April 1923

Mongols watering their camels. These wells [near Wang Yeh Fu] were dug by contract on command of the present king's father twenty or thirty years ago. They consist of a good wooden frame about the well opening, a stone or wood lining for the well itself and a watering trough made from a whole log. The Mongols keep a long pole with a bucket of basketwork hidden in some convenient spot nearby and ladle out the water to their sheep, camels, and goats as one might ladle soup on an immense scale.

Before [the wells were dug] the road was an exceedingly difficult one because of the lack of water. Now it is easy to travel over and a number of Mongols use the region for pasturage.

F. R. W.   April 1923

We came across a rich old [Mongol] lady travelling
with her brood. She wore a lovely shiny gown that
had been purple, a yellow peaked bonnet, a yellow
cloth strapped over her mouth to keep out the Kwa
Fung (blowing wind) and spectacles of horse hair
netting to keep out the dust. She rode the most
magnificent camel that I have ever seen with the
fattest, stiffest humps.

F. R. W.   April 1923

Ta Shui K'o, Great Water Gorge, a gorgeous ravine with a swift cold muddy stream running from it which spread over the plain. The stream is two feet wide and an inch deep with a velocity of two feet per second. There is ice further up the gorge. The sandy expanse outside, with thin rivulets of yellow water and the tracks of many camels, leads one to a natural gateway many yards across. Inside is a great round open space of nearly level sand, perhaps a quarter of a mile across, surrounded by red sandstone cliffs. From the upper end a gorge leads into the mountains and from it flows a swift ice-cold stream. Inside the gorge the red sandstone gives place to blue limestone veined with occasional white quartz. The passage gets narrower rapidly with rock walls closing in that can hardly be scaled and the stream bed, sometimes broad and sandy, punctuated by waterfalls. At the top of the side slopes, I could see the typical red and brown rock of the region.

F. R. W.   April 1923

We passed one caravan of 400 camels bearing wool and hides on its way in from Kansu. Each string of eight or ten had its man leading and often a dog along side. There were three babies [camels], carried on top of loads, —toothless, but already superior. An occasional farm cart broke the monotony of endless camels, dark and light, moth eaten and shaggy. Their hair is a valuable article of export and is carefully collected by the camel drivers. When it is lost the camel is extremely susceptible to cold and must be protected by blankets. The season for camel traffic is September to May. The [Han] Chinese work their beasts through the whole season and feed them regularly. The Mongol camel feeds for six months and makes only a couple of journeys a year and consequently is in much better condition and able to endure much greater hardship.

F.R.W. March 1923

Wangyefu Inner Mongolia

*Suddenly a piece of medieval wall with towers like
pagodas breaks through a gap in the trees; a few steps
more, and the whole town is in view. Wang Yeh Fu is the
capital of the Mongol State of Alashan, and I believe the
only town within its borders. The state stretches from the
Ho Lan Shan range above Ninghsia on the east to the
Edsen Gol on the west (a little river which flows down
from the mountains of western Kansu). On the south it
touches Kansu, and on the north extends "8 or 10 days
march"—probably 300 miles—into the desert. The walled
portion [of Wang Yeh Fu] is an irregular oval about 700
yards from east to west and 4 to 500 from north to south
and encloses houses and temples, the king's palace and his
garden, and the government offices. Both within and
without the walls there are extensive open spaces—inside
the walls nearly half the ground is unused—and in the
suburbs there are great numbers of large gardens. Perhaps
from 2,000 to 5,000 would be a fair estimate of the
population. The city lies in a depression, cut out by
streams in the course of time, and is surrounded by hills
which hide it on every side. Half a mile away one is
charmed by green trees and lively brooks, in striking
contrast to the sandy desert which extends many days
travel to the north and west, or the stony bare ground of
the east and south; but until fairly upon it, one would
never suspect the existence of a city.*

F.R.W. May 1923

*To the north is a commanding bluff with 3 unarmed mud
forts; to the south and southwest stretch the commercial
suburbs cut into 3 parts by streams from the bluffs to the
east. These streams give its charm to the place. They rise
from springs no great distance off, and are soon lost in the
desert, but in their short course they irrigate a hundred
gardens, and give rise to little storage pools surrounded by
high green trees. On them too, the tanners and dyers
depend and from them the town draws its water. Three
timber bridges with mud parapets carry the main street
south from the city gate through the suburbs. Most of the
people of Alashan are nomad herdsmen but most of the
working population of Wang Yeh Fu is [Han] Chinese from
Chen Fan Hsien, Kansu. Many migrate to Wang Yeh Fu
where there is a market for their labor and skill.*

F.R.W. May 1923

*It is a fairy city with its towers and pagoda, its fresh green
trees that our eyes devoured and its old lama temple of
brilliant colors and peaceful courtyards.*

J.W. August 1923

A little farm lying 4 or 5 li (3 li = 1 mile) from the mountains [outside Wang Yeh Fu]. The estate belongs to the king's uncle and is worked by [Han] Chinese under the superintendence of a friendly old Mongol.

F.R.W. May 1923

Rooftops and the king's palace inside the walls of Wang Yeh Fu.

The Manchu Yang family who lived in the southwest suburb of Wang Yeh Fu.

Boys washing and curing sheep skins.

Carpenters sawing logs of pine and spruce brought from the neighboring mountains on donkey back.

Shoe cobbler.

Wooden water buckets, the wooden frames and low doorways for the Mongols' felt tents, portable cupboards, chests and boxes, watering troughs, and readymade linings for the wells in the sand [desert] are all made by the carpenters of Wang Yeh Fu.

Mr. Mung [right], the postmaster, in all his official regalia, with one of the head lamas at Wang Yeh Fu.

A Mongol comes in from the country with his riding
camel for a day or two's shopping, leading the camel from
booth to booth as [he] bargains.

Merchants selling their goods under the trees of market square.

*Blacksmiths use the street for a workshop, setting
their anvils and forges near a house wall.*

The trumpeters who blew retreat every evening.

A p'ai-lou on the street leading to the great Lama Temple.

The Abbot of the lamasery of Choni. Gansu.

The little Tibetan village of Choni is very beautiful with wooded mountains all about, a rushing river and queer tribes people of mixed [Han] Chinese-Tibetan descent. It is the capital of a Prince, Yang Ta Run, who rules 48 wild tribes to the south of the Tao River. The dialect spoken is very peculiar. Some call it a mixture of Chinese and good Tibetan. The Prince it was told me that his people migrated here from central or western Tibet some 600 years ago.

They now live under indirect Chinese rule. The Prince governs them as hereditary sovereign and is himself responsible to the Kansu provincial authorities. The temple at Choni is a fine one though small. It has about 400 lamas. In matters of doctrine it must obey Lhasa but in all other things it depends on the Choni prince. Gansu.

F. R. W. September 1923

Every self-respecting temple has its devil dances several times yearly. They are held, I believe, to drive out evil spirits. Those at Choni are famous for the beauty and richness of the costumes, some of which cost 5000 taels, and people flock from far and near to see them. One figure wears an inane smile. He is the saint who has attained buddhahood. Nothing can make him angry. They throw rice in his face and pester him otherwise during the dances, but he grins on serene and sweet tempered. Others are fearful in greater or less degree; all of them striking. Lamasery of Choni. Gansu.

F. R. W.   September 1923

Kumbum

Rows of gaily painted prayer wheels at the lamasery of Kumbum, cylinders packed with prayers and holy formulas. To turn such a cylinder makes as much merit as if one said the prayers contained in it. The monks are ceaselessly turning them. Qinghai.

Eight Stupas that commemorate eight monks beheaded by a [Han] Chinese general who captured the lamasery of Kumbum in a period of civil disorder. They constitute the true entrance to Kumbum. Qinghai.

Young Lamas learning theological lessons in the courtyard of the great Buddhist temple at Kumbum. Qinghai.

The Lamasery of Kumbum, in the place of honor facing the
gateway, is the house of worship itself. The whole exterior, and the
galleries, are beautifully done in columns and sculptured wood,
painted in all the colors of the rainbow. Inside is a wilderness of
columns covered with bright cloth and dimly lighted from above.
The columns stand about 12 feet apart, and there are 7 bays the
long way of the temple and 4 the wide. All around the gallery is
hung with gay flags of embroidered or printed silk. The posts are
square, covered all the way up with gorgeous yellow Ninghsia
carpets that have brown dragons figured on them, and the prayer
cushions are of figured wool. Altogether, the impression is one of
height and dim splendor of coloring. Qinghai.

Labrang

The village [of Labrang] is a dirty little place, half [Han] Chinese and half Tibetan. Its architecture has no charm but its population has: a medley of lamas, wild tribesmen, [Han] Chinese fur buyers, Mohammedan soldiers and richly dressed Tibetan women with magnificent straight figures and white sheepskin hats. Many live by their charms. The monastery lies half a mile up the valley. The intermediate space is broad and fairly level. It gives one a fine view of massive buildings with gold roofs rising here and there above a regular city of low dwellings in which lamas live. To the right is a fine white stupa or t'a around which pilgrims ceaselessly perambulate. It stands at the mouth of a small side valley where dead lamas' remains are devoutly fed to the vultures. The t'a was put there, they say, to prevent floods from rushing down this valley upon

the temple. A roadway leads from the village to the temple and beyond. On it there is a ceaseless stream of lamas, pilgrims, hucksters, townsmen, idlers, soldiers and peasants, up to the temple and down again.

One comes first to long sheds filled with prayer wheels that pilgrims spin as they pass. These sheds surround the whole monastery, a circuit, they say, of 10 li [3⅓ miles]. The roadway turns past them into a broad esplanade that leads up along the Labrang River, in front of a series of minor temples and bridges to a wider space where a market is held every morning; then on past a great golden stupa to the open country again.

This morning market at Labrang is a fascinating place to shop, for here the belongings of dead lamas

and all manner of odd wares, are likely to come for sale. I bought a prayer drum made of two human skulls. Another stall had finely mounted eating knives, each with a set of ivory chopsticks in the same scabbard, another had little temple bells of bronze, another some modern rifle cartridges, stolen or smuggled, and others brass teapots, wooden tea bowls and cloth. On a hillock at the edge of the crowd stood a few wild nomads in sheepskin, holding horses. Low mud-walled buildings hide the view. One comes at last to a big open space on which face the massive buildings which are the heart of Labrang.

First among them is the great gold roofed Chanting hall. Outside it is an imposing Tibetan structure with pillared courtyard, golden hinds on the roof and richly painted doorways. Inside a glowing blaze of softened light that plays on red wood pillars, silken streamers and yellow patterned cushions for 5,000 crouching lamas. The light streams in from windows on a gallery above; and underneath this gallery, in almost total shadow, stands a long row of golden images, each with its burning butter lamps and other signs of worship.

Next to the great Chanting hall are the kitchens with copper kettles ten feet across for brewing the lamas' tea. Wooden lidded cauldrons of copper, half round on the bottom, are let into a stove of brick, stone or clay where the fire is built. Like all [Han] Chinese, Mongols, or Tibetans, these lamas are famous consumers of tea and carry their taste so far that they drink it at services. Gansu.

F. R. W.   August 1923

Labrang Lamasery. Gansu.

Monks in front of a temple where the Living Buddha of Labrang is often enthroned. Gansu.

Nomads in sheepskin. Labrang, Gansu.

*Tibetan women selling fodder in the
marketplace of Labrang village. Gansu.*

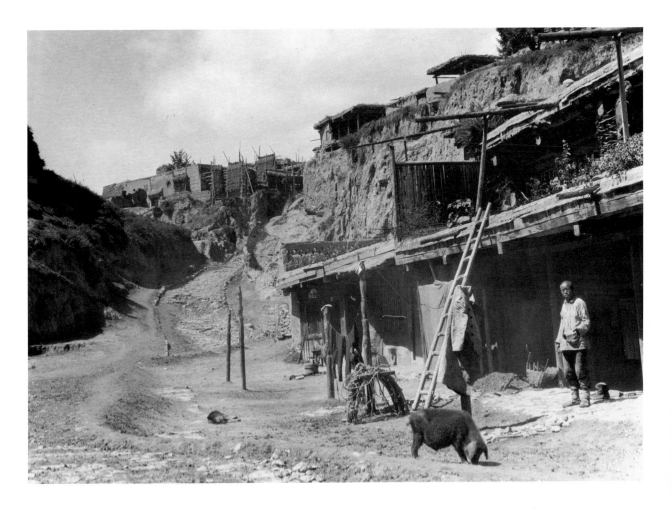

In general a Tibetan house consists of two or more rectangles of buildings each facing on a court and placed one behind the other. One or more may be two stories high, usually those toward the rear. Half of the first story will be stable sheds without walls, and part of the main kitchen is often a stable also. A ladder often leads to the roof, a pleasant resting place with a wide view.

What strikes one first is the enormous amount of wood used in construction and the comfort and charm of the houses. Nearly all the interior walls and partitions, the galleries, upstairs and down, ceilings, and often the floors, are of smooth well finished wood. A living room or a kitchen is charming and likely to be finely panelled all around, the wood stained dark and polished and often decorated with fine little paintings on the doors of

wall cupboards. Rows of shining copper pots gleam on shelves let into the wall. The house mistress stokes the big mud cooking range with dung or twigs and savory smells rise from huge wooden lidded cauldrons of decorated copper. A long Tibetan gun and sword may hang on pegs in the panels. There is a k'ang near the stove separated from it by a low railing; one's whole impression is of a Scottish baron's hall. The chief fuel at Shi Shan K'o is dung, dried in large flat cakes stacked against the sides of the houses. In other places they use wood and still others, charcoal.

Livestock is important. The people keep dogs, pigs, chickens, sheep, goats, donkeys, etc. Horses, yak and sheep are brought in through the gate at twilight, the former often to share their master's room. Gansu.

F. R. W.   September 1923

The village was all on two main streets each with gates at the end. The houses all touched each other and none had a courtyard, so the street performed courtyard functions of workshop, washroom and mule loading place for all the community. Outside was uncultivated, bare, broad valley sloping up to low mountains—the temple on one hand and a gentle meandering stream with a few trees to border it, on the other. Gansu.

F. R. W.   September 1923

Tibetans working in the fields—pretty girls with magnificent headdresses, often with their gowns dropped down to leave the right shoulder and breast bare. The hair is done in a great number of long slender braids which hang down the back to the waist. These many pigtails are caught in a frame of red cloth, nearly a foot wide, decorated with shells and disks of silver and brass which hangs down almost to the ground. The body dress is a long sleeved robe like a wrapper with a girdle of cloth or rope. When they are working the women pull out one arm or both and tie the long sleeves around the waist. All the Tibetan women's garments that I saw were on this pattern: of dirty sheepskin for the nomads, of coarse homespun or sheepskin for the peasants and of fine cloth lined with fleece for the swell beauties of Labrang. Gansu.

F. R. W.   August 1923

The people were harvesting all along our road. Men and women worked together in the fields but women predominate. They gather a handful of grain and cut it off with a short sickle, stooping over; then rise to bind the sheaf with a fast twisting motion. Gansu.

F. R. W.   September 1923

They [Tibetans] store the grain on high frames of poles where it hangs like a perpendicular thatch to dry without danger of rotting from the damp soil. Whole villages are adorned with these scantlings on house roofs and near threshing floors. From a distance it makes them look as if they were all poles. Gansu.

F. R. W.   *September 1923*

[Tibetan women] in never ending procession bring up tall wooden buckets of water from the river on their backs. Gansu.

F. R. W.   *August 1923*

We came to flocks feeding and saw black tents made of yak hair scattered in several sheltered side valleys where none had been three days before. The tents were about 25 feet square, of coarse black homespun in strips sewed together. Inside two rows of poles prop up the cloth; outside are other rows of poles and ropes and stakes. These have no proper ridge or point, they are simply great cloth lifted away from the ground over all its central part. In the center was a long mud fireplace reaching back under the roof crack which served as a chimney; in front of it, great wooden tubs for water, milk and butter; behind it, a pile of dried dung. Around the sides of the tent stand a neat double row of sacks and decorated wooden chests containing the worldly goods of the tent owners. On the grass floor lay a straight heavy sword and a long old fashioned gun with its prong. Qinghai.

F. R. W.   August 1923

The men [of Tibet] wear short cotton breeches and a knee length fleece lined coat, at least in the Hsun-Wha Labrang region, and both sexes are likely to appear in conical sheepskin hats, the brim turned high to show the white fleece inside. No travelling Tibetan man is complete without a straight clumsy sword stuck crosswise in his girdle. Gansu.

F. R. W.   August 1923

Index of Romanizations

Postal-atlas, Wade-Giles, and/or other familiar Romanizations follow the official PRC *pinyin* transcriptions when different.

Baotou = Paotow
Beijing = Peking
Beiping = Peiping

Chang Jiang = Ch'ang-chiang (Yangtze River)
Changdu = Ch'ang-tu (Chamdo)
Chongqing = Chungking

De Wang = Te Wang
Dengkou = Teng-k'ou
Dingyuanying = Ting-yüan-ying

Fanzi = Fan-tzu
Feng Yuxiang = Feng Yü-hsiang
Fengtian = Fengtien

Gansu = Kansu
Guisui = Kweisui, Kuei-sui
Guomindang = Kuomintang

Heilongjiang = Heilungkiang
Hexia = Ho-hsia
Hezhou = Ho-chou, Hochow

Jiang Jieshi = Chiang Kai-shek
Jilin = Kirin
Jin = Chin
Jinchuan = Chin-ch'uan
Jinsha Jiang = Chin-sha-chiang

Lanzhou = Lan-chou, Lanchow
Liangzhou = Liang-chou
Linxia = Lin-hsia
Liu Yufen = Liu Yü-fen

Ma Bufang = Ma Pu-fang
Ma Fuxiang = Ma Fu-hsiang
Ma Hongkui = Ma Hung-k'uei
Ma Qi = Ma Ch'i
Ma Zhongying = Ma Chung-ying
Manzhouguo = Manchukuo
Mao Zedong = Mao Tse-tung

Nanjing = Nanking
Nanzhao = Nan-chao
Nian Gengyao = Nien Keng-yao
Ningxia = Ninghsia, Ningsia

pinyin = p'in-yin
Puyi = P'u-yi

Qin = Ch'in
Qing = Ch'ing
Qinghai = Ch'ing-hai

Ruanruan = Juan-juan
Rehe = Jehol

Shaanxi = Shensi
Shandong = Shantung
Sheng Shicai = Sheng Shih-ts'ai
Sichuan = Szechwan
Song = Sung
Sun Yixian = Sun Yat-sen

Tang = T'ang
Tao = T'ao
Taozhou = T'ao-chou
Tujue = T'u-chüeh
Tuoba = T'o-pa
Turen = T'u-jen

Wangyefu = Wang-yeh-fu

Xiahe = Hsia-ho
Xikang = Sikang
Xingan = Hsingan, Hsing-an
Xining = Sining
Xinjiang = Sinkiang
Xiongnu = Hsiung-nu
Xixia = Hsi-Hsia
Xizang = Hsi-Tsang
Xu Shuzheng = Hsü Shu-cheng
Xunhua = Hsün-hua

Yalong = Ya-lung
Yanan = Yenan
Yinchuan = Yin-ch'uan
Yitiaoshan = I-t'iao-shan
Yongluo = Yung-lo
Yuan = Yüan
Yuan Shikai = Yüan Shih-k'ai
Yunze = Yün-tse
Yushu = Yü-shu

Zhangjiachuan = Chang-chia-ch'uan
Zhangjiakou = Chang-chia-k'ou (Kalgan)
Zhao Erfeng = Chao Erh-feng
Zhili = Chihli
Zhungwei = Chung-wei